THONDESWARAM

(DEVINUWARA – DONDRA)

by

Thiru Arumugam

First published in 2017 by Ohm Books, UK

ISBN 978-1973919797

Cover design and original sketch by Darshan Rajarayan being an artist's impression of what the Gal-gé (Stone Temple) at present day Devinuwara would have looked like when it was built in the seventh century.

Dedicated to the memory of Sanmugam Arumugam (1905 - 2000)
Pioneer Ceylonese Irrigation Engineer and Scholar

CONTENTS

ACKNOWLEDGEMENTS

Acknowledgements are due to the following for making this book possible.

To Ram Bharrathann for his foresight in conceiving the idea of the Pancheswaram Dance Drama in 1999 in London and bringing Thondeswaram into the limelight and persuading my father, Sanmugam Arumugam, to provide material for the lyric writers of the Dance Drama. The lyric writers in Chennai, Prof. Va Ve Su and Padmashree Lalgudi Jayaraman came back to my father asking for more information about Thondeswaram and he replied saying that was all the information that he had. I resolved then that I would one day delve deeper into the subject.

To Darshan Rajarayan for the cover design and sketch and his artist's impression of what the Galgé (Stone Temple) would have looked like when it was built in the seventh century AD, and also for drawing the Map of Devinuwara.

Thanks to the Publishers, Ohm Books, UK. Seggy T Segaran has spent many hours formatting the text and putting this publication together. If not for his encouragement and enthusiasm, this book would not have seen the light of day.

Finally, last but certainly not least, thanks to my wife Malini and the rest of the family for their continuous support and encouragement throughout the process of writing this book.

Thiru Arumugam
Sydney, Australia
August 2017

1
INTRODUCTION

Shruthi Laya Shangham (now known as Institute of Fine Arts) is a registered British Charity dedicated to the promotion of South Indian classical music and dance in the UK. On 16th October 1999, the Shangham produced a Bharata Natyam Dance Drama titled "Pancha Ishwaram of Lanka" at Logan Hall, University of London. The Dance Drama had original lyrics written by the famed violinist and composer Padmashree Lalgudi Jayaraman and Prof. Va Ve Su. The original music for the Dance Drama was composed by Padmashree Lalgudi Jayaraman. The original choreography was by Vijayalakshmi Krishnaswamy, Professor of Dance at Rukmini Devi College of Fine Arts, Kalakshetra Foundation, Chennai, India. The lead dancers were all graduates of this same College.

The theme of the Dance Drama "Pancha Ishwaram of Lanka" was a delineation in classical Bharatha Natyam dance form and lyrics of the history of the five pre-Christian era Sivan Temples of Sri Lanka. These five temples dedicated to the Supreme Lord Ishwaram (Siva) were located on four coastal sides of the country and were to safeguard the island from oceanic bed upheavals, convulsions of the earth's crust and other natural disasters that occurred during that period. The temples were Thiruketheeswaram and Muneeswaram on the west coast, Naguleswaram on the north coast, Thirukoneswaram on the east coast and Thondeswaram on the south coast. A free translation into English of the lyrics of the Thondeswaram segment of the Dance Drama is given in Appendix A. Although the history of the first four temples has been well documented in books and articles, not much information is available about Thondeswaram on the south coast.

The Civil Servant, P E Pieris, D. Litt (Cantab) is of the opinion that these temples existed before the time of Vijaya (sixth century BC)[1]:

> *Long before the arrival of Vijaya there were in Lanka five recognised Isvaram of Siva which claimed and received the adoration of all India. These were Tirukketisvaram near Mahatittha, Munnissaram dominating Salawatta and the Pearl Fishery, Tandesvaram near Mantota, Tirukkonesvaram opposite the great Bay of Koddiyar and Nakulesvaram near Kankesanturai. Their situation close to those ports cannot be*

the result of accident or caprice, and was probably determined by the concourse of a wealthy mercantile population whose religious wants called for attention. The temples in Sea Street in Colombo are a modern illustration of the operation of the same principle.

Tandesvaram near Mantota referred to above is Thondeswaram near Matara. A history of Jaffna titled *Yalpana Vaipava Malai* written in Tamil by the poet Mathagal Mailvagana Pulaver about 1736 also mentions these Sivan temples. His reference to the 6th century BC Vijaya is as follows in a translation by C Brito[2]:

He was a staunch worshipper of Siva: and began his reign by dedicating his city [the Tamil original says State] *to that god and building four Sivalayams as a protection for the four quarters of his infant kingdom:- In the East he erected Konesar-koyil at Thampala-kamam: In the West he re-built Thiruk-kethich-churan-koyil, which had long been then in ruins: In the South he raised Santhira-sekaran-koyil at Maththurai: and on the North he constructed Thiruth-thampa-lesuran-koyil and Thiruth-thampa-lesuvari-amman-koyil at Thiruth-thampalai, at the foot of Kiri-malai.*

Santhira-sekaran is another name for Siva and the Santhira-sekaran-koyil at Maththurai referred to above is the Sivan temple at Thondeswaram which is about two miles from Matara.

The Programme Souvenir[3] for the "Pancha Ishwaram of Lanka" Dance Drama written by Sanmugam Arumugam says on page 15[4]:

Recent (1998) revelation of a Shiva Linga Hindu Deity, in the South of Sri Lanka

The following news item appeared in the London popular weekly Journal "Newslanka", of 5th November 1998:

"Shiva Linga" found at Devinuwara

A sculptured 'Shiva Linga' was found in the foreground of Othpilima Vihara in the historical Vichithrama Viharaya in Devinuwara.

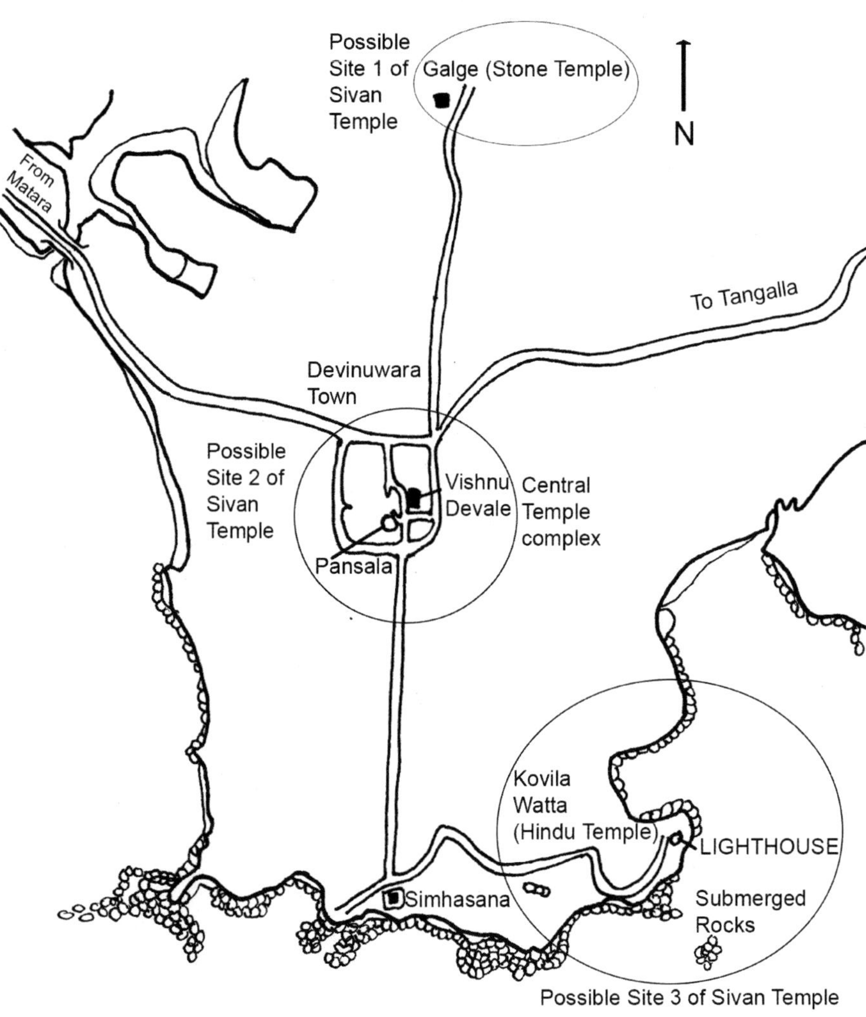

Fig 1: Devinuwara (Sketch by Darshan Rajarayan)

A person who was weeding the temple garden traced the sculpture. The 'Shiva Linga' is 4 feet in height and 2½ feet in width. At an earlier occasion too a similar sculpture was found at the same premises. It is believed that these findings give a clue as to the existence of a 'Shiva Devale' at the premises in the past."

As Hindu Temples have not been known to have functioned in that region in recent years, the unearthed Shiva Linga Murthi may obviously be a deity from one of the Thondeshwaram Temples. As the Lingam is said to be comparatively large in size, it could even be the principal Murthi of the ancient Temple.

What have been unearthed are extremely interesting. The 'avudaiyar' or the pedestal of the Shiva Lingam appears to be a thin slab; the upright or vertical portion is tall and slender. The 'Nandhi' Ishapam appears to be of a coarse finish, showing lack of suitable implements. These can therefore be said to be of very ancient origin, probably of about the Pallava era.

The 'Pallava era' referred to above would have been about the seventh century AD. The existence of the first four of the Pancha Ishwara Temples is well known and there exist Sivan Temples at these locations even today. The location of the fifth temple i.e. Thondeswaram was at the town presently called Devinuwara (City of Gods) which is at the southernmost point of Lanka. During British period it was called Dondra and the southernmost tip of Lanka was called Dondra Head. The location co-ordinates are: Latitude 5^0 55' north of the equator and Longitude: 80^0 33' east of Greenwich. A list of alternative names given to this location over the ages is given in Appendix B.

Devinuwara is on the A2 southern coastal highway. It is just past Matara on the road to Tangalle. See Fig. 1. Even though Dondra Head is north of the equator, south of this point there is no land mass until Antarctica is reached. Dondra Head is also the site of Lanka's tallest and most powerful Lighthouse. It was commissioned in 1890 and it is 49 m tall with its beams visible up to 50 km away. All materials for its construction came from UK, including the granite rock bricks. It was designed by James Douglass and constructed by William Douglass of the Imperial Lighthouse Service. In 1996 a Rs

2 Sri Lankan postage stamp was issued with a picture of this Lighthouse.

Constance F Gordon Cumming, a travel writer, who visited Dondra about 1890, wrote this about the Lighthouse in a book she published about Ceylon[5]:

> *In 1889 the Queen's* [Victoria's] *birthday was celebrated by a very different event, namely, laying the last stone to complete the finest lighthouse on the coast, one of a series extending from Colombo right round the southern coast of Ceylon as far as the 'Great' and 'Little Basses', within such moderate distances of one another so as to afford all possible security in navigation. The foundations of this latest addition to the lights of Ceylon were hewn in the solid rock at the close of 1887, the Jubilee year, and when this finishing touch was given, the summit of the tower stood 176 feet above the sea level – a lonely beacon-star for the guiding and warning of many a vessel in the years to come.*

Notes:

1. **Pieris P E,** 1917, 'Nagadipa and Buddhist Remains in Jaffna', *Journal, Royal Asiatic Society (Ceylon) Vol XXVI No.70 -1917,* pp 17-18.
2. **Brito C,** 1879, *The Yalpana Vaipava Malai or the History of the Kingdom of Jaffna,* page 3, Colombo. This is an English translation of the original 1736 Tamil text. A Tamil version was published by Mudaliyar Kula Sabanathan in 1953.
3. *Violin Trio & Dance Drama, Pancha Ishwaram of Lanka,* Logan Hall, University of London, 16th October 1999
4. The London weekly *Newslanka* newspaper was edited by the London Correspondent of Lake House, Colombo (Associated Newspapers of Ceylon Ltd.).
5. **Gordon Cumming, C F**, 1893, *Two Happy Years in Ceylon,* London, p 447-448.

2
THE DEITIES AT DEVINUWARA

The existing three storey Devale at Devinuwara, the Vishnu Divya Raja Bhavana, is a Vishnu Temple built around 1950 in the classical Kandyan style of architecture which has similarities to the Kerala style of temple architecture (see Fig. 2). However, different views have been expressed as to the original deity worshipped at this location.

Fig. 2: Vishnu Devale, Devinuwara (Photo - Thiru Arumugam)

S Paranavitana Ph.D. (Lugd.), the doyen of Sri Lankan Archaeologists and the first Sri Lankan to be appointed Commissioner of the Archaeological Survey of Ceylon, has written a full-length book on the subject of shrines at Devinuwara[1]. In the book he develops the theory (pp 19-59) that the original shrine here was that of Upulvan, but that around the 15th century or so worship of a subsidiary deity or Bow-god became prominent[2]:

> *This Bow-god was honoured at Devundara in the form of Rama, the best known among the epic heroes who wielded a bow given by Varuna. The Paravi Sandesa* [a 15th century epic poem] *also affords evidence to support the view that it was as an incarnation of the Bow-god that Rama was*

worshipped in ancient Ceylon. The cult of Rama too seems to have prevailed among the ancient Sinhalese. This secondary deity, the Bow-god Rama, gradually overshadowed Upulvan and in accordance with the religious beliefs which then prevailed in India, was taken to be the same as Visnu.

Paranavitana goes on to say that by the 16th century the principal deity worshipped here became Visnu[3]:

The fate which overtook Upulvan in the sixteenth century was similar. He had become thoroughly native and was no longer respectable. His place, therefore was taken by Visnu, a deity who commanded the allegiance of millions in India then, as indeed he does even today.

Paranavitana also postulates a connection between Upulvan and Varuna. Although worship of Upulvan by the Sinhalese has now been replaced by Visnu worship over the past five centuries, the origin of Upulvan worship goes back to the time of Vijaya, when Upulvan was given the task of guarding Lanka, though even at that time the distinction between Upulvan and Visnu is not all that clear.

The *Dipavamsa,* i.e. Chronicle of the Island, is the oldest historical record of Lanka and was compiled in the 3rd- 4th century AD. It describes the passing away of Lord Buddha as follows[4]:

21. 22. At the time, when Sambuddha, highest of men, attained Parinibbana, that son of Sihabahu, the prince called Vijaya, having left the land called Jambudipa, landed on Lankadipa. It had been foretold by the most excellent Buddha, that the prince one day would be (its) king. 23. The Teacher at that time had addressed Sakka, the chief of gods: "Do not neglect, Kosiya, the care of Lankadipa". 24. Sujampati the king of gods, having heard the Sambuddha's command, committed to Uppalavanna the business of guarding the island. 25. Having heard the command of Sakka that powerful Devaputta with his attendant demons kept guard over the island.

The *Mahavamsa,* i.e. Great Chronicle, records the history of Lanka. It was written about the 5th century AD. Geiger's translation of the portion of the Pali text which records the passing away of Lord Buddha is as follows[5]:

When the Guide of the World, having accomplished the salvation of the whole world and having reached the utmost stage of blissful rest, was lying on the bed of his nibbana, in the midst of the great assembly of gods, he, the great sage, the greatest of those who have speech, spoke to Sakka [king of the gods] *who stood there near him: 'Vijaya, son of Sihabahu, is come to Lanka from the country of Lala, together with seven hundred followers. In Lanka, O Lord of gods, will my religion be established, therefore carefully protect him with his followers and Lanka'.*

When the lord of gods heard the words of the Tathagata he from respect handed over the guardianship of Lanka to the god who is in colour like the lotus.

Geiger has added the following footnote about the last line above as follows:

Devass' uppalavannassa, that is Visnu. The allusion is to the colour of the BLUE lotus (uppala).

Ananda Guruge in his translation of the *Mahavamsa* translates the last line above slightly differently[6]:

The lord of the gods heard the words of the Tathagata and with respect entrusted the protection of Lanka to god Uppalavanna.

Guruge adds a footnote as follows[7]:

Uppalavanna, Geiger translates as 'the god who is in colour like the lotus'. Corrected by Buddhadatta and Mendis by replacing 'Lotus' with 'water-lily'. I prefer to treat it as a proper name. Malasekera says 'The god is generally identified with Visnu, though there is evidence to show that, at least in later mythology, the two gods were distinct'.

It can be seen from the above that as regards the identity of the god entrusted with the guardianship of Lanka is concerned, the translator of the *Dipavamsa* identifies him with Uppulvan whereas the translators of the *Mahavamsa* consider both Uppulvan and Visnu as possibilities.

Professor J C Holt has made an exhaustive study of the subject in a 442 page book titled *The Buddhist Visnu*. He observes that[8]:

> *I think it is more likely, as I said at the outset, that Upulvan originated as an indigenous deity in Sri Lanka and was later conflated with Visnu, rather than originating with the identity of an early Sinhala adaptation of Visnu. In other words, I think it is more accurate to invert the process that Obeysekere has described: Upulvan becomes Visnu rather than the other way around. If Upulvan's origins had to do with Visnu, there would be some traces of such a legacy in the development. But there isn't any iconographic, mythic, or ritual trail to follow to warrant this conclusion. Thus, I think that what has transpired in Sinhala Buddhist religious culture is that a sixteenth- or seventeenth century conflation between Upulvan and Visnu made possible a later adaptation and transformation of the latter. In the process, Upulvan was largely forgotten, but lives in the guise of the transformed "Buddhist Visnu".*

The Obeysekere reference above is to Gananath Obeysekere, formerly Professor of Anthropology at Princeton University, USA, and page 315 of his book *The Cult of the Goddess Pattini,* Chicago, 1984. Holt comments as follows[9]:

> *What Obeysekere has actually done here, and admits to, is to having invoked the Puranic conception of avatar, i.e., that Visnu and Upulvan are references to the same god, who assumes different forms. For Obeysekere, Upulvan is an early Buddhist "take" on Visnu, and the other Visnu referred to in inscriptions and in sandesa literature is the original god of Hinduism: there is now a "Buddhist Visnu" and a "Hindu Visnu", as it were.*

Nalin de Silva explains the difference between the "Hindu Vishnu" and the "Buddhist Vishnu" as follows[10]:

> *Even if the God Vishnu was introduced to Sinhala Buddhism later from Hinduism and merged with the God Upulvan, the God Vishnu of Sinhala Buddhism is not the*

> *same as God Vishnu of Hinduism. Hindu God Vishnu has gone through a kind of metamorphism before the God Vishnu of Sinhala Buddhism. In Sinhala Buddhism all gods are mortal beings and not eternal. The God Vishnu is a Bodhisathva* [sic] *who would become a Buddha in the future ... and is not an avathar* [sic] *of Brahman ...*

This distinction between Upulvan and Visnu is also maintained in the Kokila Sandesa (i.e. Cuckoo Message), which is a majestic Sinhala poem written in the 15th century by the Principal of a College in Devinuwara. It is in the form of a message carried by a bird and has a graphic description of the temples of Devinuwara. The translation of the relevant verse which reiterates that Upulvan and Visnu (i.e. the Lily coloured god and Vishnu) are different gods reads[11]:

> *23.* *The Lily – coloured god in glory shines,*
> *In endless prowess the mighty Vishnu's peer –*
> *Who crushed the previous gods and showed his ire,*
> *And now presides as guardian of the Faith.*

The translator W F Gunawardhana's footnote about this verse reads as follows:

> *This is the god whose sacred seat is Dondra, and to whom, at Buddha's death-bed, the care of Lanka, which, it was foreseen, would become an abiding home of the Faith, was committed by Indra, the chief of gods. By lily coloured here is meant the colour of the blue water lily, which is also the colour of Vishnu, and on that account this god is generally confused in popular idea with Vishnu himself. The confusion is heightened by the fact that nothing of the god's pedigree and history as an independent deity is known.*

Local folklore is that the image of the god floated in from the sea at Dondra and this is repeated in Verse 41 of the Kokila Sandesa[12]:

> 41. *Next Mangul-Vella pass, a lovely sheet*
> *Of snow-white sand, which looks a carpet spread*
> *By Madam Earth, the day the gracious god*
> *Of Lily Hue came here from o'er the main.*

The translator W F Gunawardhana's footnote about this verse reads as follows:

> *The god of Lily Hue, according to the tradition preserved at Dondra, came over from Southern India, in the shape of a floating log of Kihiri (Accacia catechu), and touched down first at Kirulawella, a small fishing port of Dondra. But the Kapurala or god-invoker at Sinigama near Hikkaduwa, who had been apprised in a dream, and was going with a large procession to receive the god, had not yet arrived. So the god had to put back to sea, where, rounding the Point of Dondra at Sinhasana, he floated on to Mangul-vella on the Matara side of Dondra, where on the shore he was received with all due homage by the functionary from Sinigama with his train, and carried in procession to Dondra. Mangul-vella (auspicious beach) received its name from the auspicious event of his touching.*

This wooden statue of Upulvan is believed to have escaped destruction when the Portuguese razed to the ground the temples of Devinuwara in 1587 because it had already been moved to Alutnuvara Devale in the Kegalle District. From there it appears to have been taken either to Kandy or Dambulla. There is an ancient Visnu Devalaya in Kandy, popularly known as the Maha Devalaya. Robert Knox described the deity in it as Alut Nuvara Deiyyo, indicating that it originally came from Alutnuvara.

Ulrich Von Schroeder has identified two wooden Upulvan statues at the ancient Dambulla Temple. He describes them as follows[13]:

> *Especially enigmatic is the iconography of the blue coloured Upulvan deiyo, variously identified as Varuna, Rama and Avalokitesvara, but nevertheless worshipped by the common Sinhalese as Visnu (Plates 123D-E and 124A). Of the two Upulvans at Dambulla, one is represented in an ascetic manner and one is bejewelled. Of special significance is the icon in Cave 1 in Dambulla (Plate 124A), because it bears an effigy of Tathagata Amitabha in the crown and thus correlates in every aspect with the images generally identified as Avalokiteswara. It is apparent that this sculpture possesses no similarities to Visnu.*

It is the Upulvan deity in Cave 1 (Plate 124A of Schroeder's book) that is supposed to have originated in Dondra. His description continues[14]:

> *124A. Upulvan Deiyo, Dambulla, Rajamahavihara, Cave 1, height 2.68m. This image worshipped as Visnu or Upulvan is not on view to the public and was never described or published before. It is a popular belief in Southern Sri Lanka that this image originates from the Visnu Devale at Dondra (Devundara) from where it had been taken first to Alutnuvara (Kegalla District) and then subsequently brought to the Maha Saman Devale at Ratnapura[15].*
>
> *This image now worshipped as Upulvan or Visnu deiyo, was produced in an artistic environment exposed to a strong Pallava influence. The importation of a wooden image of Visnu from India during the Pallava period is recorded in an ola manuscript discovered in the Kegalla District[16].*
>
> *In the year 712 of the Saka Varsa (790 AD), a red sandalwood image of Visnu was brought across the sea. King Dapulu Sen, after having a vision of the image, built for it a deva vimanaya at Devinuvara (Dondra). Some 183 years later (973 AD) the image known as Sri Visnu Diviya-raja was transferred to the newly built deva mandiraya at Alutnuvara (Kegalla District). The above mentioned King Dapulu Sen would be Dapula II (c815 – 831 AD) who is historically related to a restoration of a stone temple at Dondra. The Saka year 712 (790 AD) may refer to the prince whose regnal years as King Dapulu II lasted from c815 to 831 AD. The present condition of the Upulvan in Cave I is too excellent by far to date from about 800 AD, and possibly represents a replacement copied during the Polonnaruva period. It is obvious that this sculpture, which bears no similarity to Visnu, represents an emanation of Amitabha.*

If the Upulvan deity in Dambulla is not the deity that came from Devinuvara, where did the Devinuwara Upulvan deity go? Holt is undecided about its final destination[17]:

> *... there are other variants of this myth which declare that*

the "Visnu image" was brought instead to Alutnuvara in the thirteenth century, and then to Kandy (rather than Dambulla) in the seventeenth or eighteenth century (or even to Gadaladeniya or Hanguranketa, depending on which kapurala is relating the myth and where it is told).

Fig. 3: Lamp Pillar in Temple courtyard (Photo - Thiru Arumugam)

There are other writers who do not agree with Paranavitana's Upulvan – Rama – Varuna hypothesis. A D T E Perera argues at length[18] the case for Upulvan being the all embracing Mahayana Bodhisattva Avalokitesvara. Prof A Seneviratna argues the case for the god worshipped at Devinuwara being Rama[19]:

> *In the year 1516, a Siamese Buddhist monk named Ratnapanna in his work Jinakamalini enumerates the guardian gods of Sri Lanka as Sumana, Rama, Lakkhana (Laksman) and Kattagama (Kataragama). Here Rama is substituted for Upulvan while Kattagama stands for Skanda Kumara. Saman and Lakkhana are taken as two different gods, thus ignoring Vibhisana. This evidence proves beyond doubt that the god worshipped at Devundera was none other than Rama.*

In the grounds of the Buddhist temple in Devinuwara there stands a four-sided tall stone pillar (see Fig. 3), previously used as a lamp post for an oil lamp, but this function became redundant with the advent of electricity. Each of the four sides has a bas-relief carving. Paranavitana and Seneviratna have slightly different views about what the carvings represent.

One of the faces has a bas-relief carving of a figure with a head-dress, signifying him to be a god or royalty, and carved showing him discharging an arrow from a bow. Paranavitana[20] says that this may be a representation of Dunu-devu (Bow-god), but as the other three faces are decidedly Saiva in character, he suggests that this may be Siva drawing a bow called Pinaka.(See Fig. 3a). He goes on to state[21]:

> *If we have a representation of Siva on this pillar, it may possibly be the pillar on which was 'carved the figure in relief of God Hara i.e. Siva', referred to by Sri Rahula in the description of the Mavat-maduva[21]. But as the pillar has certainly been removed from its original position, this would not help us in identifying that 'Pavilion on the High Road'.*

Fig. 3a: Siva carved on Lamp Pillar (Photo - Thiru Arumugam)

Seneviratna[22] disagrees with the view that this carving is a representation of Siva. His view is that considering the literary, historical and folkloristic evidence available about the shrines at Devundara, the artist's intention was to delineate the figure of Rama.

On another face is a representation of Ganesa, and there is no difficulty in confirming the identification of this deity in this bas-relief.

The next face of the stone pillar has the bas-relief carving of a multi-faced god facing sideways, standing on a peacock and holding a drawn bow. The head of the figure is turned to his left and we are able to identify three faces on the visible side, making a total of six faces. The number of faces and the vehicle (peacock) give a positive identification and Paranavitana and Seneviratna both agree that this is a representation of Karttikeya (Skanda Kumara) (See Fig. 3b).

Fig. 3b: Skanda carving on Lamp Pillar (Photo - Thiru Arumugam)

The fourth face has the bas-relief figure of a god facing forwards and five heads are clearly visible. The figure appears to be holding a weapon, probably a spear. No vehicle is shown. Paranavitana suggests that this is a six headed figure and that the sixth head is at the back and is therefore not visible, and that this figure is also of Karttikeya. However, usual representations of Karttikeya facing forwards would show all six faces. Seneviratna does not agree that this is a six headed figure, and suggests that we can count five heads facing forward and five more may be hidden from view, making a total of ten heads. And this figure must therefore be that of the ten-headed Ravanna. The picture in Fig 3 shows Karttikeya on the right and Ganesa on the left.

Local folk lore believes that the last battle between Rama and Ravanna was in fact fought in the environs of Devundara, and that Ravanna's principal palace was here. This would support the view that two of the carvings on the stone pillar are those of Rama and Ravanna. The other two carvings are Ganesa and his brother

Karttikeya who are venerated in shrines at Kataragama. In fact, local legend has it that Karttikeya arrived from India in a Gal-pahura (granite raft), beached at Dondra and then proceeded to Kataragama by an overland route.

H E Ameresekere is of the view that the Devundara shrine was dedicated to Rama, probably soon after the battle with Ravanna[23]:

> *The principle shrine is the Vishnu Divya Raja Bhavana also known in ancient times as Santhera-Sekaram-Kovil and Naga-risa Nila Kovil. It was dedicated to Rama Chandra, the avatar of god Vishnu, the hero of Ramanaya, the Vanquisher of Ravanna, the cruel Rakshasa King of Lanka.*

The names of the temple in ancient times in the above reference is interesting and shows a connection with Siva. Santhera-Sekaram (i.e. he who wears the crescent moon on the crown) is one of the alternative names for Siva. Paranavitana points out[24] that Naga-risa Nila Kovil is a misreading by Rhys Davids[25] of a local inscription and that ‘Nila’ should read ‘Nam’ which means ‘named’. Therefore ‘Naga-risa nam Kovil’ means the ‘Kovil named Naga-risa’. Paranavitana continues to say that Isa is a well known epithet of Siva, and that Naga-risa must mean the Isvara (Siva) of Nagari, and that Nagari is a shortened form of Deva-nagari an alternative name for Devinuwara (Thondeswaram).

Other shrines here include the Kataragama Devalaya of Skanda in a separate small shrine and the seven Minor Devalayas are in seven rooms in one long building. The seven deities are Valli Matha (Skanda’s consort), Pattini, Saman, Gana Deviyo (Ganesha), Aluth Deviyo (Dadimunda?), Basnaiva Deviyo and Devol Deviyo. This building is shown in Fig 4.

Fig. 4: Seven Minor Devalayas (Photo - Thiru Arumugam)

Administrative control of the Devales is the responsibility of the Basnayake Nilame. He is neither appointed, nor is it a hereditary post. He is elected for a five year term by the votes of the 650 Grama Niladharis (formerly called Village Headmen) in the region. The persons responsible for the religious services in the Devales are called Kapuralas. It is a hereditary position and the Devinuwara Kapuralas can trace their lineage back over ten generations or more. The Kapuralas act as intermediaries between the devotees and the deities. The devotee gives a tray containing the offering of betel leaves, flowers, fruits, rice etc. to the Kapurala and tells him the nature of his problem e.g. health, financial, employment, downfall of enemies etc. The Kapurala then goes into the inner sanctum sanctorum and implores the help of the deity in solving the devotee's problem. The Kapurala chants an appropriate *yatikava* (petitionary prayer) addressed to the deity. The deity being a Bodhisattva (enlightened being) also gains merit by helping the devotee. The Kapurala retains a part of the offering and returns the rest to the devotee. The *yatikava* includes the words[26]:

> *... Maha Visnu, being known to the world by ten names such as Sankha Sila and Devanarayana, complete in ten avatars, we are seeking refuge and help from you, king of gods, who dwells here in the heavenly Devinuvara palace casting your loving glance about.*

Prof. J C Holt interviewed 324 devotees who presented problems to the Kapuralas in the Visnu Devalaya in Kandy in

February/March 2001 and recorded the proportions of the types of problems as follows[27]:

39.5%	"Blessing" (santiya) for general planetary problems
18.5%	Family (fertility, marriage, domestic violence)
14.5%	Planetary problems (specified)
12.0%	Health
7.8%	Vows for justice
7.4%	Economic prosperity
0.3%	Sorcery

Fig. 5: Simhasana (1950s) where Skanda rested (Courtesy Archaeological Dept.)

Another God associated with Devinuwara is Skanda. Local belief is that Skanda (son of Siva) crossed the Indian ocean in a *Gal-pahura* (granite raft) and landed at Devinuwara. He rested on a stone slab near the beach, called the *Simhasana,* while local residents paid obeisance to him. A shrine has been built to enclose the stone slab, which is close to the beach and about a kilometre directly south of the main temple complex. A 1950s picture of the *Simhasana* shrine with a thatched roof is shown in Fig. 5. Two stone pillars which formed part of the original temple here can be seen in the front of the picture. The thatched building has since been replaced by a permanent building which can be seen in Fig. 6. From Devinuwara, Skanda made his way overland to Kataragama where he courted and married the Veddah Princess, Valli, and he is venerated as the Kataragama Deviyo.

Fig. 6: Simhasana (restored) where Skanda rested (Photo - Thiru Arumugam)

Fig. 7: Nandhi in Temple courtyard (Photo - Thiru Arumugam)

Ancient Hindu stone sculptures in the courtyard include an image of Ganesa and another one of Nandhi, a Bull, (Fig. 7), Siva's vehicle and gate-guardian. Nandhis are usually positioned facing the main shrine in a Sivan temple. It is believed that these two sculptures were found long ago in the area known as Kovil Watta, near the Lighthouse on the sea shore, and moved to their present position in the main temple courtyard.

Another Hindu stone sculpture is that of a Siva Lingam. The discovery of this Lingam has been described in Chapter 1. The Lingam is usually the main embodiment of a Sivan temple and is placed in the most sacrosanct area of the temple in the Moolasthanam i.e. the holy of holies. Fig. 8 is a picture of this Siva Lingam which was unearthed by a gardener digging a flower bed in the garden of the Othpilima Vihara about twenty years ago. Fig. 9 is a close up of the Lingam. The proportions of the Lingam which is tall and slender, and the fact that it only has a base and no pedestal seem to indicate that it is not of the Chola period and could be early Pallava period or around 7th century AD or even earlier. At the top there is recess where there would originally was a large precious stone. The recess is surrounded by a carving of a crescent moon pointing upwards. The crescent moon is found in the locks of Siva's hair, and this Lingam may have been the holy of holies of an ancient Sivan temple at Thondeswaram.

Fig. 8: Siva Lingam in front of Othpilima Vihara
(Courtesy - Institute of Fine Arts)

Fig. 9 Siva Lingam close up
(Courtesy - Institute of Fine Arts)

Apart from the Vishhnu Devale, the Buddhist holy places here include a Dagaba which is inside a circular shrine (Vatadage), a Vihara and Pansala (Fig. 10) with images of recumbent and seated Buddha and the Othpilima Vihara, a Bo tree and a recently constructed masonry standing image of Buddha (Fig, 11) which is about the height of an adult coconut tree.

Fig. 10: Dagaba and Pansala (Photo - Thiru Arumugam)

Fig. 11: Standing masonry Buddha (Photo - Thiru Arumugam)

The possible arrangement of religious sanctuaries in this location in medieval times has been described by Paranavitana as follows[28]:

> *The references in these* [Sandesa] *poems establish that there were, in the fourteenth and fifteenth centuries, three distinct groups of sanctuaries in Devundara. The Ganesa shrine and possibly other Saiva places of worship existed on the beach. A rest-house for pilgrims was also attached to these shrines. Farther inland was the ancient vihara of the place. The third was Upulvan's shrine which, to the authors of the Sandesa, was the distinctive feature of the town. The vihara seems to have been separated from the Upulvan shrine by the town, and at a later date the Aluthvidiya was between the vihara and the Vallemadama. These three classes of holy places at Devundara are referred to in a thirteenth century slab inscription, now badly, weathered, to be seen near the modern devale. The inscription adds a fourth category of holy places (dharmaksetra), the four in order given in this document being, (1) vihara (Buddhist monastic establishments), (2) devala (shrines of Sinhalese gods), (3)*

> *kovil (shrines of Hindu gods), and (4) agrahara (area set apart for the residence of Brahmins).*

Sir Paul E Pieris lists the shrines at Devinuwara as follows. Note that he describes the Lotus hued as Vishnu, not Upulvan[29]:

> *Eight Kovilas in all occupied the place, for Kataragama and Pattini were worshipped here as well as Vishnu the Lotus hued. On emerging from the Magul Welle there stood the Vihara of Buddha; the painted Wata Dage contained the Dagoba; two images of Buddha, the Ot Pilima and the Siti Pilima, gave their names to two of the buildings; while the Pansala called the Galatura Mula Paya, with an ambulatory and Rat Pat Sulu Paya, completed the one set of buildings. But the glory of the place was the Sri Vishnu Devi Raja Bawana, with its Maha Wat Maduwa.*

Notes:

1. **Paranavitana S,** 1953, The Shrine of Upulvan at Devundara, *Memoirs of the Archaeological Survey of Ceylon, Volume VI,* Colombo.
2. Ibid, pp 57-58.
3. Ibid, p 59.
4. **Oldenberg H,** 1879, *Dipavamsa,* p 161.
5. **Geiger W,** 1912, *The Mahawamsa or the Great Chronicle of Ceylon,* London, p 55.
6. **Guruge A,** 1989, *Mahavamsa,* Colombo, p 535.
7. Ibid, p 771.
8. **Holt J C,** 2004, *The Buddhist Visnu: Religious Transformation, Politics, and Culture,* New York p 87.
9. Ibid, p 86.
10. **De Silva N,** 2000, The Political Bishops, *The Island,* February 21, 2000. Quoted by Holt (2004), Ibid, pp 408-409.
11. **Gunawardhana W F,** 1919, The Kokila Sandesa, *Ceylon Antiquary and Literary Register, Volume IV, Part III,* Colombo, p157.
12. Ibid, p 160.
13. **Schroeder U V**, 1990, *Buddhist Sculptures of Sri Lanka,* Hong Kong, p 383.
14. Ibid, p 406.
15. **Seneviratne A,** *Golden Rock Temple at Dambulla,* pp 50-51.

16. **Bell H C P,** 1904, Report on the Kegalla District of Sabaragamuwa, Colombo, pp 46-48.
17. **Holt J C,** (2004), p. 73.
18. **Perera A D T E,** 1971, Upulvan, the Patron God of the Sinhalese, *Vidyodaya Journal of Arts, Science and Letters, 4.1&2,* January/July 1971, Nugegoda, pp 88 – 104.
19. **Seneviratna A**, 1978, Rama and Ravanna: History, Legend and Belief in Sri Lanka, *Ancient Ceylon*, Colombo, p 223.
20. **Paranavitana** (1953), p 38.
21. **Wijayawardhana W R** (1925), Editor, *Paravi Sandesa,* Verse 150, Colombo.
22. **Seneviratna,** pp 224-227.
23. **Ameresekere H E**, (1931), Vimal Sri Dewunuwara, *Ceylon Literary Register, Vol. 1,* Colombo, p 199.
24. **Paranavitana** (1953), p 75.
25. Journal of the Royal Asiatic Society, Ceylon Branch, 1870-71.
26. **Holt J C**, (2004), p 222.
27. **Holt J C**, (2004), p 224.
28. **Paranavitana** (1953), pp 12-13.
29. **Pieris P E**, 1913, *Ceylon: the Portuguese Era – being a History of the Island for the Period 1505-1658,* Colombo, p 240.

3
EARLY HISTORY AND MIDDLE AGES

Local legends believe that Ravanna (circa 2500 BC), the King of Lanka, had his main palace near the Dondra lighthouse in an area which is still known as Kovil Watta. Ravanna was a Brahmin and an ardent worshipper of Siva and it is therefore probable that he would have built a temple for Siva here. Local belief is that the final epic battle between Ravanna and Rama also took place in Devinuwara, and that Rama discharged the fatal arrow that killed Ravanna from the hill overlooking the town.

The official website of the Vishnu Devalaya had this comment[1:]

> *The Temple of Vishnu is one of the oldest and most powerful temples. It is said that this devale was erected by prince Rama commemoration of his victory over king Rawana. This devale is said to be situated at the spot where king Rawana had fallen dead and the place where the present galge is said to be the spot where prince Rama took aim to shoot Rawana. This was a temple for god Shiwa.*

The 'Temple of Vishnu' referred to is the Vishnu Devale and the 'galgé' referred to is the stone temple on the outskirts of Devinuwara town which will be described later. This is corroborated in principle by an interview that Prof. J C Holt had with the Chief Kapurala of Devinuwara[2]:

> *He* [the Chief Kapurala] *acknowledged that Visnu was understood quite differently in the Hindu tradition as a creator deity with many avatars, but that he and the people of Devinuvara regarded Visnu (rather than Natha, as held in Kandy and elsewhere), as the next Buddha-in-the-making. While the Devinuvara devalaya was his chief abode, Visnu, he said, was also the chief protector of the Sri Mahabodhi in Anuradhapura and the Dalada Maligava in Kandy. He said that the nearby galgé was not the site of the original Upulvan devalaya, as Paranavitana had argued, but was instead the place where Rama had killed Ravana; and so it was simply a memorial to Ravana as a Lankan hero of the past.*

The earliest known map of Ceylon was drawn by the Greek Onesicritos. He was the Chief Pilot of one of the ships of Alexander the Great. About 327 BC he sailed on a voyage around the coasts of India and wrote the book *Paraplus or Description of the Coasts of India.* The book includes a map of Ceylon and a description of the country. In his map there is no place name given for the southernmost tip of Ceylon.

Fig. 12: Ptolemy's Map of Taprobane c150 AD.
(Courtesy - Wikimedia Commons)

The next map of Taprobane, as he called it, was drawn by the Greek Ptolemy about 150 AD. He did not personally visit Ceylon but based his map on the map by Onesicritos plus additional information obtained from seafarers who had visited Ceylon. The map is shown in Fig. 12. The southernmost point of Ceylon is marked as *Dagana civitas sacra luna* and an icon of a temple is drawn at that point to indicate that there was a major temple at that location. Prof. C Suntharalingam has this comment[3]:

> *The name Dagana appears to be a compound of D(v)a + gana, being a transliteration of the Tamil 'deva' meaning 'God' plus the Tamil 'gana' meaning 'people'. Sacrum Lunae with its variants, means 'Sacred to the moon'. The place has been correctly identified as Devendra, according to the Mahavamsa, and as Dondra Head, Devinuwara, in present day geography.*
>
> *There is in this place a very famous ancient Saivite temple dedicated to God Siva with a striking prominent Crescent Moon to signify Siva's Consort Parvathi on his head. In Tamil the image is known as Sandiramoliswarar, meaning literally 'Moon Wearer on the Head'.*

Dagana civitas sacra luna means Dagana, City Sacred to the Moon. We have seen in Chapter 2 that the Siva Lingam in the temple grounds has a crescent moon carved near the top. This would seem to indicate that the prime deity worshipped at this temple was Siva, and that Thondeswaram is one of the five recognised Iswarams of Siva mentioned by Dr P E Pieris[4].

References to this area in the ancient chronicles are listed by C W Nicholas[5]. The earliest reference to this place in the Culavamsa says that[6] Dappula, the son of Mahatissa, was appointed Yuvaraja of Rohana (circa 659 AD), and that[7]:

> *Dappula built the Ambamala-vihara and many other viharas; he also erected the Khadirali-vihara and offered to the god.* [Geiger adds a footnote that] *Presumably there was at this spot a local Hindu cult, probably of Skanda, the God of Kajaragama, a kind of patron saint of Rohana; and the King did not neglect to reverence the deity.*

Paranavitana says that Khadirali referred to above is Devinuwara[8]:

> *An eighth-century inscription, recently brought to light in the grounds of the vihara at Devundara, refers to the old monastic institution at the place by the name of Kihirali-pirivana. The name Kihirali would be Khadirali in Pali, and a Khadirali Vihara is said to have been founded by Dappula (in Sinhalese Dapulusen), a seventh-century Prince of Rohana, who made an unsuccessful bid for the*

> *throne of Anuradhapura.* [Paranavitana explains on pp 60-61, the inscription referred to above] *The epigraph is an edict of Apa Kitakbo granting immunities to lands dedicated to a monastic institution named Kihirali-pirivena at Giriyala ... 'Giriyala', obviously, is an older form of 'Girihela', which the Paravi Sandesa (v. 195) gives as the name of the abode of Upulvan. It has, therefore, to be taken as the ancient name of Devundara ... 'Giriyala' and 'Kihirali' thus appear to be identical.*

This establishes beyond doubt that Dappula built a Vihara at Devinuwara about 659 AD. C W Nicholas says that[9]:

> *The Sinhalese Chronicles ascribe the foundation of Devnuvara or Devunuvara Vihara first to Dappula (Dapulusen), then to Aggabodhi IV (667-683), and finally to Manavamma (684-718).*

The Sinhalese historical chronicle, the Rajavaliya, gives credit to an earlier king, Sri Sangabo, as the builder of Devinuvara and also mentions Dapulu[10]:

> *Thereafter King Lamini Dalapatissa renovated the already existing Viharas and reigned nine years. His nephew, king Sri Sangabo built the Siyagal Vehera and the city of Devenuvara and reigned sixteen years with the help of the God-king. After him, king Valpitivasi descendant of the Okkaka clan reigned ten years. After him, Hunannaru Riyandala reigned six months. The son of the aforesaid king Pasulukasabu* [i.e. Dapulu], *went to the port of Dharmahal and taking a powerful army from the country of Kasavatti, came back and having killed king Hunnannaru Riyandala captured back the kingdom. He caused to be built the Devnuvara and constructed eight tanks and reigned thirty-five years.*

The next reference to Devinuwara is in 790 AD in an Ola manuscript discovered in the Kegalla district by H C P Bell, the first Commissioner of Archaeology (*Report on the Kegalla District,* pp 46-48, 1904). This is quoted by H E Ameresekere[11]:

> *On the full moon day in Vesak, in the Saka year 712 (790 AD) a red sandalwood image of Vishnu was brought across the sea. King Dapulu Sen saw in a vision that the image had started and would be landed at Girihelapura, Magulwella; and it was told him that he must build a dewa-vimanayak in Dewunuwara. Accordingly, the King built the city of Dewunuwara as ordered, and kept there the red sandalwood image of Vishnu, and in the month of Esala planted the sacred post (kap-hitawanawa) at a lucky hour as customary before the commencement of the perahera, and commenced the procession. In it the image of Maha Brahma was borne ahead; this was the origin of such processions in the Island. The place was called Vimal Sri Dewunuwara.*

Vikkamabahu I (1029-1040 AD) ruled Rohana and visited the town of Devinuwara when he had raised an army to attack the Colas who were ruling large parts of Ceylon, but he fell ill and died there. According to the Culavamsa[12]:

> *What boots me the ceremony of raising of the umbrella* [i.e. consecration] *so long as the possession of the Rajarattha is not achieved? Then the mighty (Prince) assembled a hundred thousand men. But as at the time when the campaign should have begun, he was suffering from the wind disease, he thought it not the time to carry on war and entered suddenly in the twelfth year (of his reign) into the city of gods* [i.e. Devinuwara] *and came into the company of the gods.*

Vijayabahu I (1055-1110 AD) restored the Devanagara Vihara. According to the Culavamsa[13]:

> *… the vihara called Uruvela and the vihara in Devanagara* [here Geiger adds a footnote that this can also be translated as] *… the vihara called Uruvela in Devanagara, … these and many other viharas which had fallen into decay, the Sovereign restored and granted villages to every one of them.*

The grant of a village to a vihara means that the revenue and taxes from the village can be used for the maintenance of the vihara.

Parakramabahu I's (1153-1186) troops fought a major battle in Devinuwara against the troops of Queen Sugala during his conquest of Ruhuna. This is recorded in the Culavamsa[14]. Ameresekere quotes Ancient Inscriptions of Ceylon, 138, to say that Parakramabahu I gave gifts to Devinuwara[15]:

> *1186/7. In the tenth year of his Majesty Siri Sanga Bo Parakrama Bahu a coconut tope bought for a tumba (?) of gold to the Bhumi maha wihara and to the image house, and two hundred coconut trees to the Lord Dewaraja. Let those who increase these gifts and uphold their continual inheritance, enjoy the bliss of release in heaven. Those who enjoy the fruit of these trees ought, from time to time, to plant seedlings.*

C W Nicholas states that Nissanka Malla who reigned from 1187 to 1196 visited Devinuwara and had the temples there repaired[16].

About 1244 during the reign of Parakramabahu II (1236-1270), a Javaka King invaded Lanka with his troops. Parakramabahu II sent his sister's son Prince Chandrabhanu with troops to repel the invaders. After several hard fought battles, Chandrabhanu routed the invaders. The Culavamsa says that[17]:

> *After thus putting to flight the Javakas in combat, he* [Chandrabanu] *freed the whole region of Lanka from the foe. Hereupon he betook himself to Devanagara, worshipped there the lotus-hued god* [Geiger in a footnote says this is a reference to Visnu] *and celebrated for him a divine sacrifice. He had erected there a privena that was intended for the Order; it received the name of Nandana, since it was the delight of the people.* [Geiger adds a footnote] *… here for the first time we have a notice of the shrine of Visnu celebrated in the Middle Ages … It is significant that Virabahu offered his sacrifice of victory in a Hindu sanctuary… At the same time however, he builds a parivena for the Buddhist Order, thus putting his attitude towards their parity beyond a doubt. Even today a Hindu devalaya and a Buddhist vihara stand side by side in Dondra.*

In 1250 AD, Parakramabahu II visited Devinuwara and restored the whole temple. He also initiated the asala perahera which is held about July. This perahera has been held there ever since and this year it will be 761st annual perahera, making it by far the oldest annual perahera in Lanka, far older than the Kandy Perahera. The Culavamsa describes the work of Parakramabahu II as follows[18]:

> *Then when the monarch learned that in the sacred town of Devanagara which was a mine of meritorious works, the shrine long since erected to the lotus-hued god – the King of the gods, had now fallen into decay, he betook himself to the superb town and in rebuilding the dwelling of the King of gods like to the heavenly mansion of the King of gods, he made of it an abode of all riches. Then the best of men had the town filled with all splendours even as the beauteous city of the gods. Hereupon he determined to celebrate every year in the town an Asalhi festival for the god.*

Parakramabahu IV who reigned from 1302 to 1326 visited Devinuwara around 1325. He built an image house and four stone gates with elaborate carvings. The gate frame is high enough for an elephant to pass through during a perahera procession. One of these gate frames is still standing and can be seen in Fig 13. The Culavamsa record of his visit is as follows[19]:

> *In Devapura he built a long temple consisting of two storeys, provided with four pairs of gates for the image of the recumbent lion. To this temple he assigned the grove-encircled village Ganthimana* [now known as Gatamana] *by name which he proclaimed as the property of the Buddha.*

Ibn Battuta (1304-1368?) was a Moroccan who was one of the world's greatest travellers. In his life time he visited most of the countries which at that time had a significant Muslim population. In 1325 he left home at the age of 21, ostensibly on a pilgrimage to Mecca. It turned out to be a 24 year journey in which he visited Lanka in 1344. He visited Adams Peak and Devinuwara. His observations on the latter are[20]:

Fig. 13: 14th century Stone Gate Frame (Photo - Thiru Arumugam)

... the town of Dinewer, a large one, built near the city and inhabited by merchants. In a vast temple is seen an idol bearing the same name as the town. In this temple there are upwards of a thousand Brahmins and djoguis [yogis] *and about five hundred women, born of idolater fathers, who sing and dance every night before the statue. The town and its revenue are the private property of the idol; all who live in the temple and those who visit it are supported therefrom. The statue is of gold and the size of a man. In place of eyes it has two large rubies, and I was told that they shine at night like two large lamps.*

During the reign of Bhuvaneka Bahu IV (1341-1351) his Prime Minister and brother-in-law Sena-Lamkadhikara sent much wealth, such as pearls and gems to Devinuwara and built a three storied image house for a standing image of the Buddha[21].

Vijayabahu VI commenced his reign in 1510 and the University of Ceylon's *History of Ceylon* refers to a Saiva Kovil in Devinuwara as follows[22]:

> *At Devinuvara, there was a Saiva Kovil named Nagarisa, to which benefactions were made in the reign of Vijayabahu VI by a personage named Vendarasakonda-perumal, a captain (aracci) of the body-guard (atapattu).*

Note that the University of Ceylon's *History of Ceylon,* which is the definitive work on the subject, refers to a "Saiva Kovil named Nagarisa" thereby showing that Rhys Davids' interpretation of the word in the inscription as 'nila' is incorrect and the correct interpretation is 'nam' meaning named.

By about the fourteenth and fifteenth centuries Devinuwara had reached the peak of its fame as a religious destination. As a place of pilgrimage, it was second only in popularity to Adams Peak.

Notes

1. Official Web site of the Devinuwara Sri Vishnu Devalaya, www.devinuwara.org/shrine.html, accessed on 24 July 2007.
2. **Holt J C,** 2004, *The Buddhist Visnu: Religious Transformation, Politics, and Culture,* New York, pp 354-357.
3. **Suntharalingam Prof C,** (1969), *Ancient Taprobane – Modern Ceylon: Essays on Early Geographical History,* p 38. Unpublished Manuscript.
4. **Pieris P E,** 1917, 'Nagadipa and Buddhist Remains in Jaffna', *Journal, Royal Asiatic Society (Ceylon) Vol XXVI No.70 -1917,* pp 17-18.
5. **Nicholas C W,** (1959), Historical Topography of Ancient and Medieval Ceylon, *Journal of the Ceylon Branch of the Royal Asiatic Society,* New Series, Volume VI, Special Number, 1959, pp 70-71.
6. **Geiger W,** (1929), Translator of *Culavamsa being the more*

recent part of the Mahavamsa, London, Chapter 45, verses 38 to 52.

7. Ibid, Ch. 45, V. 55-56.
8. **Paranavitana S,** 1953, The Shrine of Upulvan at Devundara, *Memoirs of the Archaeological Survey of Ceylon, Volume VI,* p 1, Colombo.
9. **Nicholas** (1959), p 70.
10. **Suraweera A V**, (2000), Translator of *Rajavaliya: A comprehensive account of the Kings of Sri Lanka,* Ratmalana, p 54.
11. **Ameresekere H E**, (1931), Vimal Sri Dewunuwara, *Ceylon Literary Register, Third Series, Vol. I, 1931,* pp 199-204.
12. **Geiger** (1929), Ch. 56, v. 4-6.
13. Ibid, Ch. 60, v. 58-64.
14. Ibid, Ch. 75, v. 47.
15. **Ameresekere**, p 201.
16. **Nicholas** (1959), p 70.
17. **Geiger** (1929), Ch. 83, v. 48-51.
18. Ibid, Ch. 85, v. 85-89.
19. Ibid, Ch. 90, v. 94-95.
20. **Ameresekere**, p 202.
21. Ibid.
22. **University of Ceylon**, *History of Ceylon, Vol. 1, Part II,* p 768.

4
THE GAL-GĒ (STONE TEMPLE)

About one kilometre north of the Vishnu Devalaya, on top of a hill, there stands a small temple built entirely of stone. See Figs 14 and 15. This temple is called Gal-gé (Stone-house or Stone-temple).

Fig. 14: 7th century Gal-ge (Stone Temple)
(Photo - Thiru Arumugam)

Fig. 15: 7th century Gal-ge (Stone Temple) side view
(Photo - Thiru Arumugam)

Col. Colin McKenzie (1754-1821) was a Scottish Army Officer who spent most of his working life in India ending up as the first Surveyor General of India. During his life-time he collected thousands of Indian manuscripts, translations, coins and paintings which were acquired after his death by the India Office Library. He was in Ceylon in 1796, the year that the British invaded Ceylon, on an assignment as Commanding Engineer and visited Devinuwara. He described the place as "Ruins of a Hindu Temple (or Dewullum) on Dewunder-head, or Divinoor, (called in the charts Dunder-head) the Southerly point of Ceylon". He describes Galgé as follows[1], with the word Carnatick meaning South India:

... we went by a path winding among the woods about three-quarters of a mile distant, gradually ascending to the face of a rising ground, where we found a small pagoda or dewul, built of hewn stone, flat roofed, square, with one door and having no spire, pillar or arches; it had no sculpture except some mouldings about the pediment cornices, and the door; nor did any altar, image or decoration appear to shew the object of worship; though from its exact likeness to the plain style of some of the small pagodas built of hewn stone in the Carnatick, there can be little doubt of its origin.

The conservation or reconstruction of this ancient shrine was carried out by the Archaeological Department in 1947, as the building was collapsing[2]. It was described as the most important conservation of an ancient monument ever undertaken by the Department outside ancient Rajarattha. The building was deteriorating rapidly so it was necessary to dismantle it completely and reconstruct it according to the original design. Some stone slabs were missing so the gaps were filled with brick masonry and covered with a composition to imitate stone.

S Paranavitane, the first Ceylonese Archaeological Commissioner has written a comprehensive book on the subject of the Galge[3] titled *The Shrine of Upulvan at Devundara.* The shrine is of modest dimensions with two rooms, with a total length of 26 ft. 5 in. There are two doors but no windows. It faces east, as is customary in Hindu temples, so that the rising sun shines through the doorway and awakens the sleeping deity in the garbha-grha (moolasthanam or sanctum for the holy of holies). The garbha-grha is of square shape measuring 16 ft. externally and 9 ft. internally. This means that the walls are 3 ft. 6 in. thick. The reason for such strong walls would have been that above the roof there would have been a vimanam (sikhara) sitting on the flat stone roof, as is standard practice in Hindu temples. This vimanam must have been made of brick and no longer exists, but traces of its bottom layer can be seen on the roof in Fig. 16. This is confirmed by Paranavitana[4]:

> *The method adopted for the roofing of the garbha-grha, differing as it does from the ante-chamber, indicates that this roof required additional strength to carry a weight which the roof over the ante-chamber had not to bear. It is likely, therefore, that originally there was a sikhara marking the sanctum, and that the ante-chamber had a flat roof.*

Fig. 16: 7th century Gal-ge (Stone Temple) showing base of Vimanam (spire) on roof (Photo - Thiru Arumugam)

Major J Forbes who visited the Galge about 1840 also thought that there was formerly a structure above the flat roof[5]:

> *... a quarter of a mile farther inland is situated a stone building called Galgana, consisting of two rooms; the roof as well as the walls are of hewn stone, and exhibit excellent specimens of masonry. On the top there appears formerly to have been a dagoba; but the ruin is now covered with shrubs*

and creeping plants that find root in the interstices of the building.

The garbha-grha connects through a doorway to an ante-chamber, which in turn has a doorway which is the entrance to the shrine. The ante-chamber is 14 ft. 9 in. wide externally and is therefore slightly smaller than the garbha-grha. The ornamentations are confined to the doorways, there are no sculptural ornamentations on the exterior of the building. There are no niches of any kind. The corbels in the inner chamber are plain with a diagonal cut. This type of corbel is found in the early Chola temples, about 850 AD onwards, whereas the fluted corbels in the ante-chamber are a later development, leading to speculation that the ante-chamber was built later than the garbha-grha. The area surrounding the Galgé has been levelled off. It is therefore possible that the Galgé was the sanctum of a large temple, the rest of which was built of timber and has not survived. There are no inscriptions on the walls or on any stones nearby to give a clue as the type of deity that was revered in the sanctum. The outside cornices have at regular intervals, dormer like ornamentations, called kudus in Dravidian architecture. On each side of the building there eight kudus, on the front and back there are four kudus each.

11th-cent. Chola
Tanjore

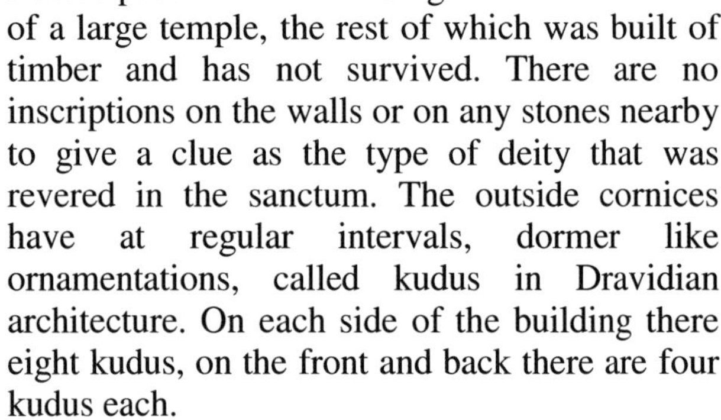

Dondra Galgē

The shape of the kudus is shown on the diagram. (Courtesy Paranavitana, 1953, p 10). For comparison, a 11th century Chola kudu is also shown. This shows that the Galge kudus are in a early stage of development compared with the 11th century Chola kudus. This would seem to indicate that Galge was built well before the 11th century.

All-stone medieval temples are not common in Lanka. Paranavitana makes this observation[6]:

Free-standing edifices of any importance, constructed entirely or mainly of stone, so far known in the island, are those dating from periods of Tamil rule, for instance, Saiva shrines at Polonnaruva [11th century], *or – when they had been raised at the command of Sinhalese rulers – due to*

> *inspiration from South India, as in the case with the shrine at Gadaladeniya* [14th century]. *They thus represent phases in the evolution of Dravidian architecture, not that of the Sinhalese.*

The art of building all-stone temples in India commenced around the seventh century AD. Building of the stone temples in Tamil Nadu in Mamallapuram, formerly called Mahabalipuram, started in the seventh century, with construction of the Shore Temple commencing at the beginning of the eighth century, and Sri Lanka would have had recourse to that experience when required, but says Paranavitana[7]:

> *That this practice has not been followed in the case of Galgé at Devundara may be due to fact that, at the time of building this edifice, the canons of Dravidian architecture had not yet been crystallized, and the master builders of that school had not yet established a reputation outside the Tamil land. If the above reasoning is justified, we can assume that the Galgé at Devundara dates from about the seventh century.*

If Paranavitana's reasoning is accepted, it makes the Galgé by far the oldest all-stone temple in Sri Lanka. In a book that Paranavitana wrote nearly twenty years later, Paranavitana repeats his conclusion that the Galgé dates from the seventh century[8]:

> *On various architectural grounds, we may assume that the Galgé dates from about the seventh century. A comparative study of styles leads one to assign it a date earlier than the Chola epoch.*
>
> *The above conclusion, which has been arrived at solely on architectural grounds, is borne out by literary evidence furnished principally by the Mahavamsa, Pujavaliya, Parakumbasirita and the Sandesa poems, from which the original founder of the shrine seems to have been the Rohana prince, Dapula.*

This would make the Galgé marginally older than the Pallava Shore Temple in Mamallapuram and the Kailasanatha Temple in Kanchipuram, both in Tamil Nadu.

E R Ayrton, the Archaeological Commissioner visited

Dondra in 1914. He wrote some diary notes about his visit which included a paragraph about Galgé. He is convinced that there was a brick spire (Vimanam) above the roof of the building[9]:

> *On the hill behind the village of Dondra is the Gal-gé. A small Vishnu (?) Devale in good condition; had this cleared of roots and jungle. Owing to the wall being double with rubble between, roots growing in the rubble have forced off the outer face on the west side. The brick spire has completely disappeared. The doorways slant.*

The cover of this book is an artist's impression of what the Galge would have originally looked like when it was first built with the vimanam.

Notes:

1. **McKenzie, Capt. C,** Remarks on some Antiquities on the West and South Coasts of Ceylon; written in the year 1796, *Asiatic Researches, Volume VI,* London, 1801, pp 425-454.
2. Administration Report 1947, Archaeological Survey of Ceylon, Section F, pp I, 9-10.
3. **Paranavitana S,** 1953, The Shrine of Upulvan at Devundara, *Memoirs of the Archaeological Survey of Ceylon, Volume VI,* Colombo.
4. Ibid, p 7.
5. **Forbes, Major J**, 1841, *Eleven years in Ceylon, Volume 2,* London, p 178.
6. **Paranavitana**, 1953, p 9.
7. Ibid, p 10.
8. **Paranavitana S,** 1972, *Glimpses of Ceylon's Past,* Colombo, p 105.
9. **Ayrton, E R**, Antiquities in the Southern Province, Diary of the late Mr E R Ayrton, Archaeological Commissioner of Ceylon, with notes by John M Senaveratna, *Ceylon Antiquary and Literary Register, Vol VI, Part 3, pp 151-152, January 1921, and Part 4, pp 191-197, April 1921.*

5
THE SANDESA KAVYAS

Sandesa Kavya (Message Poetry), started as a Sanskrit form of poetry around the fifth century AD. Perhaps the best exponent of this form of poetry was Kalidasa (5th century) who is widely regarded as the greatest poet and dramatist in Sanskrit. In a Sandesa poem, a messenger, it could be a bird, bee, cloud, wind or even a person, carries a message from one person to another. The poem describes the place where the message originates, then describes places of interest along the journey such as palaces, temples, parks, streets, countryside etc and finally describes the destination and hands over the message to the recipient.

This form of poetry spread to other Indian languages and finally became popular in Lanka around the 14th and 15th centuries. In Sinhala Sandesa poems, the messenger is usually a bird. There are four Sandesa poems which provide information about Devinuwara.

The Mayura (Peacock) Sandesa was written by Pandit Kaweeshwara in the 14th century. The destination of the Peacock is Devinuwara and the message requests Upulvan to protect the reigning monarch King Buwaneka Bahu V, his queen and various dignitaries. It relates various details about Devinuwara. The text of this Sandesa has not been well preserved.

The Tissara (Swan) Sandesa was also written in the 14th century and was written to bless King Parakrama Bahu V by Upulvan. It includes information about Devinuwara. The original text of this Sandesa is also not well preserved.

The Kokila (Cuckoo) Sandesa was written in the 15th century by the Principal of the Irugalkula Pirivena in Devinuwara. The messenger commences its journey in Devinuwara and carries a message of congratulation to Prince Sapumal, the adopted son of King Parakrama Bahu VI who was ruling in Jaffna. The poem is considered to be one of the most majestic in the Sinhala language, and the messenger traverses the length of the country starting from the southernmost point, Dondra Head, and ends in Jaffna.

Paranavitana summarises the start of the journey of the messenger, the Cuckoo as follows[1] in Devinuwara. The poem begins with a description of the town and the Cuckoo is conducted to the shrine of the god. After paying homage to the god, the bird enters the vihara, worships at various holy places and spends the night in a mango tree. In the morning, the bird wends its way along the New

Street and then south to Vallemadama which is on the beach. From there the Cuckoo continues its journey.

Verse 11 of the translation of Kokila Sandesa describes Dondra as follows[2].

> 11. K*now Dondra is this place, this city fair,*
> *Where stately mansions, bright as Meru, shine;*
> *Where gems and coral show in plenteous store,*
> *In princely shops adorning lively streets;*
> *Where lotus blows in orchards e'er in bloom,*
> *And strains of music fill the balmy air.*

Verse 12 continues the description. The Translator has added a footnote that the 'King of gods' refers to Indra.

> *12. With moat her anklet, rampart jewelled zone,*
> *High portals arms, the sun and moon ear-drops,*
> *This city, lady fair, doth e'er sustain*
> *The King of gods a diadem on her brow.*

Verse 16 mentions the god Siva. The translator adds a footnote about the last two lines "The reference is to the celestial Ganges, which, flowing from the great toe of Vishnu, is received on the head of Siva in order to break the force of the fall. It wanders about the tangled locks of Siva until it issues out as a crystal stream on top of Kailasa in the Himalayas, whence it finds its way to earth".

> *16. White flags surmounting the crystal mansions here,*
> *Tossed in the breeze, the beauteous sight present*
> *Of numerous falls from the celestial stream*
> *Meandering in the maze of Siva's locks.*

There is another reference to the god Siva in verse 20. The translator has added a footnote "The crescent moon is worn by Siva as an ornament to his brow. Here the poet suggests that the crescent Moon, which was the loveliest object of its shape, has been eclipsed by the foreheads of the maidens of Dondra, and is therefore now serving the great god Siva in order that, by divine favour, it may regain its original position of superiority". This connects with Ptolemy's reference to Dondra as "City sacred to the Moon" referring to the crescent moon in the hair of Siva worshipped here and also the name of the temple of Siva here given in the Yalpana

Vaipava Malai as Santhira-sekaran-koyil, the reference to the god with the crescent moon in his locks.

20. See long-eyed maids. Their narrow foreheads clear
Eclipse the graces of the crescent Moon.
And hence, meseems, the crescent Moon's resort
To Siva's brow – to mend its fortune still.

Verses 18, 40 and 31 describe the dancing girls in the temple. Ibn Battuta has mentioned that there were five hundred of them who sang and danced every night in front of the idol.

18. Fair maidens here in endless graces shine,
Their raven tresses bright with jasmine bloom,
Their necks with pearls, their breasts with sandal balm,
Their faces beaming like the autumn moon.
They are the glory of the mind-born god;
Like golden vines they glitter and they glow.

40. In New Street, maids behold, whose slender frames
Most delicate and soft, superbly shine,
Their faces fresh as lotus flowers new-blown,
Their palms transfixing, by their tender glow,
Their eye, therewith their heart, of gallant swains,
As tender leaves invite and hold the deer.

31. At even-tide, when damsels at his fane,
With golden bells resonant round their feet,
Like thankful bees around a bounteous flower,
Have done their nautch, then duteous enter thou.

Verse 21 refers to Vishnu.

21. Here, in this city, all ten virtues shine;
All wealth abounds. In charm 'tis like the conch
In Vishnu's hand – most blessed sight to see.
No other object will compare sustain.

Verse 28 refers to Lakshmi, the eternal consort and sakthi (energy) of Vishnu and goddess of wealth, health, fortune and prosperity. The verse refers to her embracing the 'godhead' therefore the idol of the temple must be a Hindu Vishnu.

28. As shadows in the western sun, still grow
This godhead's fortunes; Lakshmi holds him still
In fond embrace. But see the moon, with spot:
It waxes or declines with varying phase.
Be e'er so great in glory, will the moon
Thus stand compare with this illustrious god?

Verses 23 and 41 about the 'The Lily-coloured god' i.e. Upulvan, have already been quoted in Chapter 2. Verse 23 clearly shows that Vishnu and Upulvan were different gods. There is one more reference to the 'god of Lily Hue' in verse 32. The phrase 'yclept the former gods' refers to the elephants being given the names of the Asuras, who were the possessors of heaven before they were deposed.

32. In awe behold the god of Lily Hue,
The lion strong that broke the frontal knobs
Of elephants yclept the former gods,
And made his glory shine like rows of pearls
Of loveliest ray, around the muses' necks.
Salute his lotus-feet, and take thy leave.

Verse 42 has a reference to Ganesha, the elephant headed god. Ganesha is widely revered as the remover of obstacles, the patron of arts and sciences and the god of intellect and wisdom. As the god of beginnings, he is honoured at the start of rites and ceremonies. The reference to Vellemadam, the Beach Hospice, is probably the stretch of beach now known as Madam-valla.

42. *At Vellemadam, see the radiant glow*
Of rubies cast on shore by ocean-wave.
These shine like lamps in loyal homage lit
To wise Ganesha, Counsellor divine.
A thousand charms beside here greet the view.
This is a place like Part of Indra's Heaven.

Verse 30 has a reference to Buddha, described as the 'Teacher'. The god referred to is the god of Lily-Hue. The translator has added a footnote as follows "Mara, a great and powerful god, came as the Tempter to prevent the Buddha just going to be, from attaining a position which would destroy his (the Mara's) empire, i.e.

the empire of the senses. Allurements failing, he tried weapons of force though without effect. Most of the gods who had assembled to witness the attainment of Buddhahood, had fled; but the poet says that the god of Lily-Hue stood undaunted and plied his bow".

When, on the diamond throne, the Teacher sat
Of endless Bliss, and Mara came to war
Undaunted stood this god, his circling bow
In play. What need of words his prowess to tell?

Verse 34 also has a reference to Buddha, described as the 'Sage'. The description is of what can be seen in the great Vihara in the centre of the city.

There icons of the Sage, installed in shrines
Touched by the painter's hand with tender skill,
Resplendent glow. Salute their lotus-feet,
That Bliss be thine, where life's revolving wheel
Of birth and death, and birth and death again,
Will be at rest – where ends all heat and toil.

As the final stop in his outward journey from the town, the Cuckoo is enjoined to visit the Naga-Kovil. The translator has added a footnote as follows "After attainment of supreme enlightenment, the Buddha spent seven weeks in perfect rest in the vicinity of the spot where the great struggle had been gone through. The sixth of these weeks he passed inside a 'silver palace' made of the coils of the great body of Muchalinda, sheltered from sun and dew by the hood of the great cobra spread above". It is noted that the poet calls the temple a 'Kovil'. It is therefore possible that there was also an idol of Vishnu since he is often depicted as resting on the snake Adi-Shesha, the first king of all the nagas.

There, on the South, see Naga-Kovil famed
For serpent-king with wide expanded hood,
Who, by his form, proclaims great Muchlind,
The first pious member of the hooded race,
Within whose ample folds, 'neath open hood,
The Sage, in serene rest, passed week the sixth.

Fig. 17: Ancient Stone Ganesa in Temple courtyard (Courtesy - Archaeological Dept.)

The fourth Sandesa which has information about Devinuwara is the Paravi (Dove) Sandesa, written by the poet and eminent scholar Thotagamuwe Sri Rahula about 1445. The bird journeys from Kotte to Devinuwara and gives a detailed description of the destination. Paravanavitana has given a summary of the flight of this bird[3]. The bird arrives in the evening and spends the night in a hospice near the beach adjacent to a Ganesa shrine. This shrine, is in an area which is even now called Kovil-watta, was built by a merchant prince from India named Rama-candra. The stone sculpture of a Nandhi (Bull), Siva's vehicle and gate-guardian, shown earlier in Fig. 7 was discovered here. Also discovered here is a stone sculpture of Ganesa (Fig. 17) which is now in the main temple courtyard. This sculpture is badly weathered and could well be of the same age as the Siva Lingam and the Galgé i.e. seventh century.

The bird is awakened at dawn by the music of the morning pooja in the adjacent Ganesa shrine and is then asked to visit the following shrines in the main temple complex: the Dagaba, the Bo-tree, the Shrine of the Recumbent Buddha, the Shrine of the Seated Buddha, and the building where the elders of the temple resided. The bird then spends the rest of the day admiring the architectural beauty of the town and at dusk arrives at the main shrine the Raja-Gé (Kings House) when the ritual dance of the girls would begin. Sir Paul Pieris CCS, who had a D. Litt. Degree from Cambridge University, has said that the verse in the Paravi Sandesa which describes the dancing girls is the finest description of temple dance in Sinhala. The translation is as follows[4]:

With flowers entwined in the tresses of their hair,
And garlands pendant from their necks,
The women dance, as dances the budding leaf
Of the mango twig to the music of the breeze.

The information contained in the Sandesas, though limited, enables us to imagine what this temple complex was like in its heyday in the Middle Ages.

Notes:

1. **Paranavitana S,** 1953, The Shrine of Upulvan at Devundara, *Memoirs of the Archaeological Survey of Ceylon, Volume VI,* Colombo, p 12.
2. **Gunawardhana W F,** 1917 and 1919, The Kokila Sandesa, *Ceylon Antiquary and Literary Register,* July 1917, Vol III, Part 1, pp 13- 18, and January 1919, Vol IV, Part III, pp 157-161.
3. **Paranavitana**, pp 11-12.
4. **Pieris, P E**, 1913, *Ceylon: The Portuguese Era, being a History of the Island for the Period 1505 – 1658,* Colombo, p 240.

6
THE STONE INSCRIPTIONS

A total of six inscriptions on stone have been discovered so far, in and around Devinuwara, which are relevant to the history of the place. Paranavitana has published the text, transliteration and translation of all of them[1]. They will be presented in historical date order, as far as can be ascertained.

I

This stone inscription was found in the premises of the temple and is now in the Colombo Museum. The stone is 2 ft. 4 in. in height, 1 ft. 2 in. wide and 8 in. thick. The writing is in Sinhala. The first published translation of the inscription was by T W Rhys Davids, CCS in 1872. He was later Professor of Pali in the University of London and founded the Pali Text Society. The inscription is about the grant of a coconut grove for the benefit of the vihara and of Vishnu. His translation of the inscription is as follows[2]:

> *In the tenth year of the overlord (Chakrawarti) Siri Sanga Bo Sri Parakrama Bahu ...near to the Bhumi-maha and ... cocoanut tope* [stupa] *to the image house, and 200 cocoanut trees to the lord Dewa Raja (Vichnu). Let those who increase these gifts, and maintain their unbroken succession obtain the bliss of release in heaven. Those who enjoy the fruit of these trees ought from time to time to plant seedlings. People who pick up the fruits ought to present them to Nila (Vishnu).*

Regarding the name of the King, Rhys Davids says that Turnour lists nine kings with the name Parakrama Bahu but none with the prefix in the inscription. Rhys Davids quotes verse 82 of Raja Ratnakara which says “His nephew the younger Siri Sanga-bo, the king, built the Piyangul and other viharas established the king of gods at Dewnuwara”. Suraweera’s translation of the Rajavaliya (p 54) says that this king reigned for sixteen years and Rhys Davids fixes the date of the inscription as 712 AD. On the other hand, the list of kings given in the University of Ceylon’s *A Concise History of Ceylon* (p 343) shows Siri Sangabo reigning for sixteen years from 667 to 683.

Paranavitana's translation[3] differs from Rhys Davids in certain aspects. He says that the script is about the same stage of development as inscriptions of Sirisangabo Sri Parakramabahu VI who ruled from 1412 to 1467 and the inscription may be from that period but adds that "this question cannot be decisively settled". Rhys Davids says that 'Dewa Raja' refers to Vishnu but Paranavitana translates it as the 'divine king'. Nor does Paranavitana agree that the inscription ends with a reference to Vishnu.

II

This roughly dressed stone is near the Bo-tree adjacent to the vihara in the temple complex. Paranavitana says[4] it is 3 ft. 8 in. above ground and 1 ft. 3 in. wide. It is written in Sinhala, possibly of 9th century style. It is an edict of the monarch Apa Kitakbo (Kittaggabodhi in the Culavamsa) who grants immunities to villages dedicated to the Kihirali-pirivena at Giriyala. Giriyala is an older form of Girihela and is the ancient name of Devinuwara.

Although Paranavitana has given his translation of the inscription, the Archaeological Department has published nearly fifty years later another translation of the inscription based on a better estampage, except for the last three lines which have been completely obliterated. The Department's translation reads as follows[5]:

> *This Attani pillar was set up by the command of Adipada Kittaggabodhi at Giriyala vehera Devinuvara to the effect that the officials attached to the royal household shall enter (the villages named) Pasal, Keyal, Magula and Udu-mahagamuva, which are attached to (the vihara); should the householders of this village commit any one of the Five Great Crimes, the monks (of the vihara) and arbitrators shall sit in session, and after deliberations shall levy a permissible fine.*

There is a major difference between the two translations. Paranavitana's translation says that 'officials of the royal court are not to enter the lands' whereas the above translation says that 'officials attached to the royal household shall enter'. It is likely that the word 'not' has been accidentally omitted in the above translation, since the inscription is a grant of immunities. It has not been possible to determine what are the 'Five Great Crimes'.

On palaeographical grounds, the inscription has been assigned to the ninth century AD. Prince Adipada Kittaggabodhi was the Governor of Rohana and the son-in-law of King Dappula II, who reigned from 815 to 831. Although it is customary to state the regnal year of the king in an inscription it has not been done here. All that can be said is that the date of the inscription is probably between 815 and 831 AD.

III

This is a large inscription with 53 lines of text. It is standing in front of the Visnu Devale. The above ground height is 5 ft. and the width is 1 ft. 11 in. The lettering is on the front and the back. There are drawings of a sun, moon and stupa on the front and a drawing of a stupa on the back. The text is in Sinhala with a few lines in Elu, an older form of Sinhala. A detailed description and translation of this inscription has been given by Paranavitana[6].

The inscription says that it was done during the reign of King Parakrama Bahu II (1236-1269) and is testified in the last line by Deva Patiraja. We have already seen in Chapter 3 that Parakrama Bahu II built a Pirivena here called Nandana (The Delight) because it gave delight to the people. The Culavamsa devotes the whole of Chapter 85 to the construction work carried out by Deva Patiraja for Parakrama Bahu II including building religious venues and bridges[7].

The inscription is considered to be of great historical importance as it is regarding the levying of imposts at the sea-port, and detailed regulations regarding imported goods and condemns acceptance of bribes by royal officers. All this indicates that the port here must have been very busy with ships arriving from many foreign countries.

The inscription starts off by praising Lord Gautama, then praises Parakrama Bahu II, the Supreme Lord of the Three Simhalas, and then continues as follows[8]:

> *At Tendiratota, including Devinuvara, (lands which are) religious endowments of old shall be duly maintained. Apart from the maha-pandite, other persons guarding the seaport shall not intervene. Apart from the levying of such imposts as have been approved by the maha-pandite, illegal imposts shall not be levied. To those coming from foreign countries, means shall not be afforded to avoid the payment of imposts and duties that are due – which they do by*

establishing places of business, corrupting the royal officers by means of presents, and keeping with friends the merchandise smuggled from their own countries. Any object of whatever sort shall not be accepted without paying its value in money. Guarantees shall not be given to anyone coming from the port to give a property of the samgha without taking something in return and without making due inquiries.

Should anyone, who was friendly in days gone by, come towards Lamka, (penalties involving) loss of property, loss of limb, or loss of life shall not be inflicted or cause to be inflicted on anyone whomsoever on that account. Should any (charge of) guilt arise in the days to come, punishments shall not be inflicted or cause to be inflicted, for the mere reason that a charge of guilt has arisen, without investigating in accordance with the evidence and establishing the guilt.

Improprieties shall not be caused to holy places such as viharas, devalas, agraharas and kovils. Should there be offerings, and festivals conducted on behalf of the Three Jewels, or repairs necessary on dilapidated buildings, they shall be duly carried out.

Having established all these regulations so that they may continue to be observed so long as the sun and the moon continue to exist, this edict on stone has been set up so that these laws be maintained without violation by members of the samgha, the maha-pandite, those of the ten services, courtiers of the royal palace, and kings of the lineage. To that effect, I, Deva Patiraja, do testify.

IV

This inscription was found by the Provincial Engineer of the Southern Province in 1910 forming part of a culvert. It was rescued and is now in the Colombo Museum. It is unique and one of a kind. It is unique because it is in three languages with lists of gifts of similar but not identical content. The three languages are Chinese, Persian and Tamil. A detailed description of the inscription has been given by Paranavitana[9].

It is 4 ft. 9 in. high and 2 ft. 6 in. wide. All three language inscriptions are on the front of the slab, the back of the slab is bare. The Tamil inscription consists of twenty-four lines. The inscription states that it is dated in the seventh regnal year of the Chinese Emperor Yung Lo of the Ming Dynasty. Although he favoured Confucianism, he treated all religions on an equal footing. This gives the inscription a date of about 1411. The inscriptions give details of similar gifts in all three languages. The Chinese inscription gives details of gifts described as oblations to the Buddha and a "List of Alms bestowed at the shrine of the Buddhist temple in the Mountain of Ceylon as offerings". The Persian portion of the inscription is badly worn out but the theme seems to be similar to the Chinese and Tamil inscriptions. The word Islam is decipherable and this suggests offerings to Allah, Prophet or some Muslim Priest. The Tamil inscription gives a list of similar gifts to the Lord of Tenavarai in the kingdom of Lanka. Tenavarai is the Tamil form of the Sinhala Devunuwara (Sanskrit Deva-nagara, English Dondra).

So why would the Emperor of China send such valuable gifts to Ceylon? Although the Chinese Emperor Yung Lo favoured Confucianism, he treated all religions on an equal footing. He was very keen to acquire the Tooth Relic. He sent his Admiral Ching Ho with a fleet of 62 ships to Lanka, some of the ships were the largest wooden sailing ships built. Ching Ho arrived in Lanka with the three sets of gifts listed in the inscription and negotiated with the monarch of the Southern Kingdom, Vira Alakesvara for the Tooth Relic. Vira Alakesvara refused to hand it over, whereupon Ching Ho kidnapped him and carried him off to China. He was to be returned to Lanka only if the Tooth Relic was handed over. Meanwhile Parakrama Bahu VI took over the vacant throne and he was not interested in negotiating for the return of Vira Alakesvara. The Chinese realised they would not be successful and sent Vira Alakesvara back but he did not regain the throne.

The translation of the Tamil inscription is given below[10]. Note the references to Tenavarai-nayanar and Tenavarai-alvar. Nayanar would be a Saivite reference and Alvar would be a Vaishnavite reference. This is clear confirmation that there was in Devinuwara in the fifteenth century a Saivite Temple as well as a Vaishnavite Temple, with the Saivite Temple taking precedence as nayanar is mentioned three times and alvar mentioned once.

Hail … The great king of China, the supreme overlord of kings, the full-orbed moon in splendour, having heard of the fame of the Lord, presents (the following) as offerings, in the hand of the envoys Ching-Ho and Wang Ch'ing Lien to the sacred presence of the Lord of Tenavarai-nayanar in the kingdom of Ilanga.

(And he also) causes this utterance to be heard. 'All living beings who exist in this world are protected, in happiness, by the compassion of the Lord. Men, whencesoever they come thither, have their obstacles (to happiness) removed through the divine grace of Tenavarai-nayanar'. So (the following) are presented as offerings to Tenavarai-alvar; to wit, gold, silver, tulukki, silk, sandalwood and oil for anointing.

The various offerings, in detail, are:- One thousand kalancus [5 kg] *of gold, five thousand kalancus* [25 kg] *of silver, fifty pieces of tulukki* [silk] *of different colours, four pairs of banners embroidered with gold thread and (adorned with crystal), two pairs of the same red in colour, five copper vessels of antique copper for keeping incense, five black stands, ten copper vases for holding flowers, ten black stands, five wick holders for standing brass lamps, six pairs of lotus flowers made of wood and gilt, five gilt caskets for putting agil in, ten pairs of wax candles, two thousand five hundred katti of oil and ten pieces of sandalwood.*

These, included in the list as enumerated, are given as offerings to the sacred presence of the Lord Tenavarai nayanar.

The second month of the seventh year of Yung Lo.

That this inscription stone was originally in Devinuwara is supported by the writing of Portuguese Father Fernao De Queyroz in 1692[11]:

Half a league beyond Matara there was a Pagode, which next to Trincomalee was one of the greatest resort in Ceylon, where are found stone pillars which the Kings of China ordered to be set up there with Letters of that nation as a token, it seems, of their devotion to those idols.

The translator, Father S G Perera has added a footnote here 'An inscription was discovered in 1911'.

V

This inscription was found in a village called Naymmane (Naimmana) about two miles north of Devinuwara and is now in the Colombo Museum[12]. It is about 3 ft. high and about 1 ft. wide. The text is mainly in Tamil with the last two verses in Sanskrit using the Grantha script. Grantha is a script used by Tamil speakers to write Sanskrit. The script of the inscription is attributable to the fourteenth and fifteenth centuries.

The inscription says that it was written 'in the year opposite the 20th year of His Majesty Siri Parakkirama-vagu'. There is no further evidence as to which of the Parakrama Bahus is referred to, but on paleographical grounds it can be taken to be Parakrama Bahu VI who ruled from 1412 to 1467.

The inscription records the grant of the village where it was found, that is Naymmane, to the maintenance of charity towards twelve Brahmanas at the Alms Hall of the King of Gods. The inscription starts off with the usual salutation to the King and the translation continues as follows[13]:

> *Should there be any persons who have thought of anything detrimental to this (benefaction), they would suffer the consequences of the sin of having slain cows and Brahmanas on (the banks of) the Ganges. Those who shall cause the maintenance of this will obtain Heaven and Final Liberation.*
>
> [The transliteration of the Tamil text of the previous sentence is "Idu nilai ittu-k-kuduttavar svargga-moksam peravum".]
>
> *For the maintenance permanently of charity towards twelve Brahmanas at the alms-hall of the illustrious King of Gods, Sri-Parakrama-bahu, the sovereign Lord of Lamka, granted the pleasant village named Naymmane. Should there be any who, from time to time, cause the maintenance (of this grant), to them shall there be prosperity through the favour of the King of Gods. Should there be, on the other hand, any who would obstruct it through greed, they, the meanest (among Men), shall be deprived of merit, affluence and fame.*

VI

T W Rhys Davids was a member of the Ceylon Civil Service and was posted to the Southern Province. One evening, in 1870, he was at Dondra Head sitting on some rocks and watching the sunset when he noticed that as the sea receded due to the tide, there was a rock in the sand which was a uniform rectangular slab. On closer inspection, he found that there was an inscription on that rock. The rock was duly rescued and is now in the Colombo Museum.

The inscription ends rather abruptly. Either the engraving was not completed or the last few lines have been totally obliterated. The slab is 4 ft 6in. in height and 2 ft. in width. The text is in Sinhala of the fifteenth and sixteenth centuries.

The inscription gives its date as the fifth regnal year of Sirisangabo Sri Vijayabahu Cakravartti (Vijayabahu VI) who ruled from 1510 to 1521 from Kotte. The inscription records the names and extants of lands which were the property of a shrine named Nagarisa-kovil.

Rhys Davids translated the inscription and published an article about it. His translation was copied and published by Edward Muller also[14]. Paranavitana has also studied the inscription and published his own translation[15]. Paranavitana says that Rhys Davids has made an error in his translation in saying 'granting to the Nagarisa Nila temple in Dondra'. Subsequent commentators have taken the word 'Nila' meaning blue to be a reference to a Vishnu or Upulvan temple. Paranavitana points out, however, that the word in the inscription after Nagarisa[16] is 'nam' not 'nila' and that the translation should read a ' kovil named Nagarisa at Devinuwara'. He says that Nagarisa is a reference to Siva and that since the word 'kovil' is used in the inscription it must be a reference to a Hindu temple, if it was a Buddhist temple the word used would be devala. Paranavitana explains[17]:

> *This shrine has hitherto been taken to be the same as that of Upulvan at Devundara, and in the erroneous reading Nila after Nagarisa has been found a reference to Visnu. But the two syllables occurring after Nagarisa read nam, 'named'. The shrine of Upulvan is nowhere referred to in Sinhalese literature as a kovil, which term even today is restricted in its use to shrines of gods worshipped by Tamils and adopted from them by the Sinhalese Buddhists. The shrines of gods who have been naturalized among the Sinhalese are devala's.*

> *The name Nagarisa is of the same formation as Kadiresa and Konesa. Isa, the second member of these componds, is a well known epithet of Siva, and the first member stands for a place-name. Kadiresan is the God Isvara of Kadira-gaman (Katara-gama) and Konesa is Isvara of Kona-malai. Similarly Nagarisa must stand for Isvara of Nagari, which is the shortened form of Deva-nagari. The shrine on the sea coast at which this inscription was set up, has to be taken, therefore as Saiva and as being quite distinct from the abode of Upulvan.*

Paranavitana's translation of the inscription is as follows[18]. The inscription ends abruptly and is possibly incomplete. It begins with a salutation to Vijayabahu VI 'overlord of Sri Lamka' and continues:

> *Fields (of the sowing capacity of) twenty amunas of sprouted seed in Paravasara, as they appertained to the shrine (kovil) named Nagarisa at Devinuvara from the beginning, fields (of the sowing capacity of) five amunas from Pategama in Navadunna, and the allotments included in Paravasara which were brought by Vendarasa-konda-perumal, the Captain of the Body-Guard, from the Department of Royal Villages – (all these lands) were settled (as belonging to the kovil) so that offerings and observances to the god may be maintained without cessation … from those included kings, great ministers of kings, heads of provinces, and trustees of the temple …*

The interpretation 'kovil named Nagarisa' suggests the possibility the Nagarisa is a contraction of Nagara Iswara and the reference is to a 'Temple of Siva in the Town'. Since two Siva Lingams were found, this might mean there was a second Sivan Temple outside the town.

This completes the description of the inscriptions relevant to Devinuwara that have been found so far. Inscription IV establishes that there was a temple of Siva, Inscription V speaks of charity towards twelve Brahmin (priests) resident in the Alms-Hall and Inscription VI re-confirms that there was a temple of Siva.

Notes:

1. **Paranavitana S,** 1953, The Shrine of Upulvan at Devundara, *Memoirs of the Archaeological Survey of Ceylon, Volume VI,* Colombo, pp 60-80.
2. **Rhys Davids T W**, 1872, Dondra Inscription, *Indian Antiquary, Vol. 1, Nov. 01, 1872,* Bombay, pp 329-331.
3. **Paranavitana**, 1953, p 78-80.
4. Ibid, pp 60-63.
5. **Archaeological Survey of Ceylon**, 2001, *Inscriptions of Ceylon, Vol. V, Part 1,* Colombo, pp 1-3 & 415.
6. **Paranavitana,** 1953**,** pp 63-70.
7. **Geiger W,** (1929), Translator of *Culavamsa being the more recent part of the Mahavamsa,* London, Chapter 86.
8. **Paranavitana,** 1953**,** pp 69-70.
9. **Paranavitana** S, 1933, The Tamil Inscription on the Galle Trilingual Slab, *Archaeological Survey of Ceylon: Epigraphia Zeylanica being Lithic and other Inscriptions of Ceylon, Vol III, 1928-1933,* London, 1933, pp 331-341.
10. **Paranavitana S**, 1933, pp 336-337.
11. **De Queyroz, Fernao**, *The Temporal and Spiritual Conquest of Ceylon,* translated by S G Perera, Colombo, in three volumes, 1930. p 35. The original book in Portuguese was written around 1692.
12. **Paranavitana S**, 1953, pp 70-74.
13. Ibid, p 74.
14. **Muller E**, 1883, *Ancient Inscriptions in Ceylon,* London, p 140, Inscription No. 163.
15. **Paranavitana S**, 1953, pp 74-78.
16. Ibid, p 76.
17. Ibid, p 75.
18. Ibid, pp 77-78.

7
DESTRUCTION BY THE PORTUGUESE

In 1505 a Portuguese fleet landed in Colombo unintentionally, blown there by adverse winds. The Portuguese found that there were possibilities of trading with Lanka and returned some years later and set up a trading post in Colombo. At the beginning their interest was in trading, mainly cinnamon, but as the years went by they began to have territorial occupancy ambitions as well and established a fort in Colombo.

In June 1587, King Rajasinghe I ruling from Sitawaka attacked the Portuguese by starting a siege of Colombo. Meanwhile the Portuguese sent an appeal for help to Goa and by February 1588 they were able to repel the siege. During the siege, the Portuguese decided to distract the attention of King Rajasinghe's troops by sending ships to attack, loot, pillage and burn places in the south coast right up to Devinuwara. As De Queyroz records[1]:

> *Thome de Souza de Arronches, Captain-Major of the sea, sailed out with 120 soldiers in four foists* [ships], *burnt many laden vessels, took prizes and captives, and burnt the Pagoda of Tanauare* [Devinuwara].

Joao de Barros (1496 -1570) was a Portuguese Historian. The King of Portugal commissioned him to write a series of volumes titled 'Decades of Asia' covering the history of Portugal in India and Asia. He completed three volumes before he died. After he died, Diogo do Couto (1542-1616) took on the task of completing the series and wrote nine more volumes. He was a soldier in Portuguese India and he wrote the portion of the "Decades of Asia' that covers the Portuguese attack of Devinuwara. The relevant portions covering Ceylon were translated and edited by Donald Ferguson[2].

Do Couto's description of the Portuguese attack on Devinuwara starts by describing the beauty of the temple complex[3]:

> *And as our people continued victorious, they were not willing that there should escape the pagoda of Tanaverem half a league from this city, the most celebrated and most resorted to by pilgrims of all the island, excepting that of Adam's Peak, the which in structure resembled a beautiful city, having a circuit of a full league.*

> *The body of this pagoda was very great, all vaulted above, with much workmanship, and around it many most beautiful chapels, and above the principal gateway it had a very high and strong tower, with the roof all of copper gilt in many parts, the which stood in the midst of a square cloister, very beautifully and finely wrought, with its verandas and terraces, and in each square a handsome gateway for its entrance, and all around was full of flower pots, delicate flowers and fragrant herbs for their pagoda* [In Portuguese, 'pagoda' means idol as well as temple, here it means idol] *to enjoy himself when they drew him in procession along that way. This pagoda has within the enclosure very fine streets, in which live persons of every occupation, and chief of these is of women dedicated to the service of the pagoda.*

The Captain-major of the fleet then started preparing his armada for the attack on the temple complex but a violent storm erupted delaying his plans. He found the heathen lascarins (sailors) in his ship chattering among themselves and upon inquiring he was told that[4]:

> *Those heathens were glad, because their pagoda* [idol] *had hastened to maintain his honour; and that knowing that the Portuguese were going to insult him, he had sent that storm to chastise them. This superstition was a very ancient one amongst them …*
>
> *Thome de Sousa, as soon as the Christian lascarins related this to him, swore to destroy that pagoda, in order to rid the imagination of the heathens of that superstition, so that they may see how deceived they had been, and the little that their idol could do: and so when the tempest was past, on the next day in the morning he put in to land, and went ashore, giving the van to Rodrigo Alvres, and with them Miguel Ferreira Baracho, and Domingos Pereira arache; and the first thing they did was to attack a tranqueira* [junk] *that they had on the beach on a hillock, the which our people took by force of blows to the hurt of the enemy; and leaving some soldiers to guard it, Thome de Sousa proceeded to march on the city which they attacked with great determination; and the inhabitants, not trusting in the guardianship of their pagoda,*

on seeing the Portuguese, abandoned the city, and betook themselves inland.

Thome de Sousa and his 120 soldiers then proceeded to destroy over a thousand images of gods, looted the store-houses of all the valuables, slaughtered cows in the temple sanctums in order to desecrate and defile them, and then set fire to all wooden buildings and structures including the seven-storeyed wooden car (called a *theyr* in Tamil) used to convey the idol around the town during temple festivals. Finally, the cannons were trained on the brick and stone buildings to reduce them to rubble. Do Couto describes the destruction as follows[5]:

Our people proceeded to enter it without encountering any resistance, and reaching the pagoda broke open the gates, and entered it without meeting with anyone to resist them, and went all around it to see if they found any people; and seeing that all was deserted, Thome de Sousa delivered it over to the soldiers that they might do their duty: and the first thing that they employed themselves was to destroy the idols, of which there were more than a thousand diverse forms, some of clay, others of wood, others of copper, and many of them gilt.

Having done this, they demolished the whole of that infernal structure of pagodas, destroying their vaults and cloisters, knocking them all to pieces, and then proceeded to sack the storehouses, in which they found much ivory, fine clothes, copper, pepper, sandalwood, jewels, precious stones, and ornaments of the pagodas, and of everything they took what they liked, and to the rest they set fire, by which the whole was consumed.

And for greater insult to the pagoda, they slaughtered inside several cows, which is the most unclean thing that can be, and for the purification of which are required very great ceremonies.

And they also set fire to a wooden car made after the manner of a towered house of seven stories, all large and most beautiful, lackered in diverse colours and gilt in many parts, a costly and sumptuous work, which served to convey the

principal idol on a ride through the city to which likewise they set fire, by which the whole was consumed.
Upon this our people retired laden with prizes.

And as Rev. S Gnana Prakasar says[6]:

Having thus satisfied their intemperate greed and religious zeal – a strange combination often met with among the Portuguese of those days – the marauders sailed back to Colombo.

Fig. 18: Some of the hundreds of stone pillars at Devinuwara (Photo - Thiru Arumugam)

When the dust settled, all that remained standing were one of the four stone Gateways, the Galgé stone temple which was beyond the reach of the Portuguese cannon, and over two hundred stone pillars, some standing, some fallen. These are all still there today. The stone Gateway and the Galgé were already seen in Figs. 13 and 14 respectively and some of the stone pillars can be seen in Fig. 18.

Annexed to the **Pagode of Deunara** otherwise Tennavare.

185 ortas with 4,600 coconut trees.

Viria Namby Mutiar,
Liena Arache, Ranasingua Arache, Alacon Arache, Calu Arache Lascarin.
Surep guery Bramane,
Belalas 5
Carea Pescadores, 41. They paid 43 larins Amgabada originally to the Pagode and later to the King.

Chatims, 2¦
Chanda, 8
Moor, 3
Lascarin, 5
Chunambeiro, 2
Medidor, 1
Culle, 4
Pareas, 3
Mainato, 8, some described as pintor in addition.
Drummer, 3 ; Peruma Panequia
Dancer, 10 ; Apu Panequia, Verasegra Panequia, a woman Ponny ; another " sister of the Parea."

Alfayate, Tailor, 1 Rama
Trumpeter, 1
Cortador, Porovakaraya, 17
Fundidor, caster, 1, Locuruva
Goldsmith, 7
Blacksmith, 6
Turner, 9
Carpenter, 12 ; Pagatra Acharea.
a few without description, and widows.

All these orginally served the Pagode of Tennavare, and under the Portuguese their duties were transferred to Mature. The Padre at Tennavare held 3 ortas, 860 palms yielding 8,000 nuts ; he obtained 3 lr. from 3 Chandas ; 10 lr. from the Careas as Pieda ; 9 lr. from 20 widows who make Orraca. All the inhabitants of the Aldeas subject to the Pagode pay the Banaca 75 larins yearly as Uhamdiram (huvandiram).

Xaros of the Pareas of Tennavare, called Beruvaye Bada

This was paid by 48 people to the King ; they are of various villages, which are named. The highest payment is 3 larins, of which there are several instances. Among the designations appear Viradua, Acharia, Naquata, Sacalea, Baranea, Ulavalia, Tamdiria, and Liena Arache.

Fig. 19: Littoral - List of staff at Devinuwara, 1593

The Third Book of the Portuguese Tombo (Land Register), dealing with the littoral areas, that is, sea ports and villages along the coast from Puttalam to the Pagoda of Tenavare, consisting of 336 folios is preserved in the Bibliotheca Nacional in Lisbon, Portugal where it was examined by Sir Paul E Pieris. The Tombo furnishes a clear picture of the districts as they were when King Rajasinghe I of Sitawaka died in 1593, five years after the Pagoda of Tenavare was sacked. The relevant page reproduced in Fig. 19 shows some of the staff attached to the Pagoda of Tenavare who were transferred to Matara by the Portuguese[7]. The word 'Aldeas' in the Tombo means villages.

The Portuguese subsequently built a large church with three naves on stone columns on the site of the razed Pagoda. The Portuguese Historian, Father Fernao De Queyroz, writing about this place almost hundred years later says[8]:

> *There was afterwards in that place a church of the Religious of St. Francis transforming the worship of Vixnude* [Vishnu?] *Vira Jurica into the worship of the true God. On this spot the Kinglets in times past had their Court, calling it Janura* [Devinuwara] *which means 'City of God'. The Portuguese called it Tanauare from the name of a neighbouring village in which lived the dancing girls of that Pagoda.*
>
> *The word Tanauare is also a corruption of the Portuguese, for the proper name must be Natan-uare which means in that language 'come and dance'. Here is done very good casting work in copper, silver and gold, and at the mouth of the river are made muskets and spears for the use of the arrayals.*

Fernao De Queyroz lived and worked in Goa for 53 years and died there in 1688. He completed the manuscript of his book *The Temporal and Spiritual Conquest of Ceylon* before he died. Meanwhile by 1658 the Dutch had completely ousted the Portuguese from Ceylon. Queyroz was convinced that the Portuguese loss of Ceylon and massacres of Portuguese by the Dutch was retribution by god for what the Portuguese had done to Ceylon[9]:

> *... I will here point out the injustices, violences and wrongs, which the Portuguese there committed, a most sufficient justification for the chastisement which God inflicted on them.*

The Portuguese Commander of Jaffna, Oliveira, had bragged that in the Jaffna Peninsula alone he had razed 500 Hindu Temples to the ground[10].

Notes:

1. **De Queyroz, Fernao**, *The Temporal and Spiritual Conquest of Ceylon,* translated by S G Perera, Colombo, in three volumes, 1930 p441. The original book in Portuguese was written around 1692.
2. **Ferguson D**, 1908, The History of Ceylon, from the earliest times to 1600 AD, as related by Joao de Barros and Diogo do Couto, *Journal of the Royal Asiatic Society, Vol 20, No. 60,* 1908. Translated and edited by Donald Ferguson.
3. Ibid, p 373.
4. Ibid, p 374-375.
5. Ibid, p 375.
6. **Gnana Prakasar S**, 1924, *A History of the Catholic Church in Ceylon: Period of Beginnings 1505-1602,* Colombo, p 231.
7. **Pieris P E**, Litt. D. (Cantab), 1949, *The Ceylon Littoral 1593,* Colombo, p 87.
8. **De Queyroz, Fernao**, *The Temporal and Spiritual Conquest of Ceylon,* translated by S G Perera, Colombo, in three volumes, 1930. p 35. The original book in Portuguese was written around 1692.
9. Ibid, p 1005.
10. **Gunasingam Dr M**, 2008, *Tamils in Sri Lanka: A Comprehensive History (300 BC – 2000 AD),* Sydney, p 152.

8
POST-PORTUGUESE PERIOD TO PRESENT TIMES

Some years after the Portuguese destruction, the Kandyan King Rajasimha II who ruled from 1629 to 1687, recaptured Devinuwara from the Portuguese, demolished the Church and re-built the Vishnu Temple and Viharas.

Fig. 20: Portuguese drawing of Temple at Devinuwara, 1650.

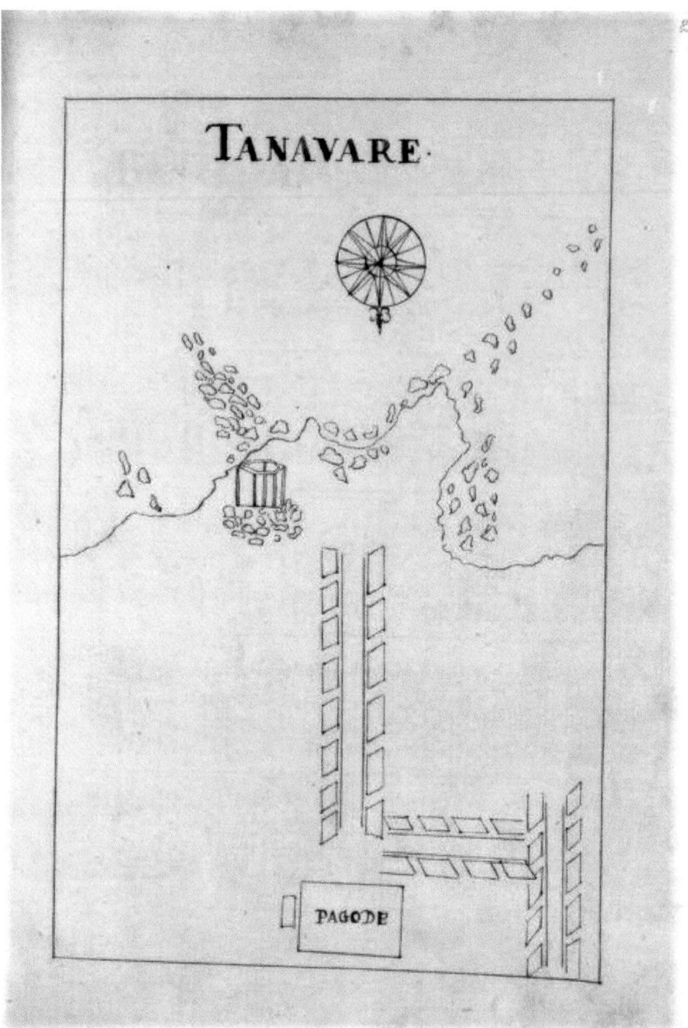

Fig. 21: Portuguese Devinuwara Site Drawing, 1650.

In 1926, Sir Paul E Pieris published a book titled *Portuguese Maps and Plans of Ceylon, 1650.* This book was based on a Portuguese manuscript held by the Library of Congress, Washington DC. This book has a drawing of the front elevation of the Pagoda at Detanavare (Devinuwara). The book also has a site plan of Tanavare (Devinuwara) which shows the location of the Pagoda. It also shows a stockade near the beach, but this was built by the Dutch. Since the manuscript gives a date of 1650, the Pagoda shown must be the one built by Rajasimha II mentioned above. The two drawings are shown in Figs 20 and 21 respectively.

Paranavitana's comment on these drawings is as follows[1]:

A Portuguese map of Devundara published by Dr Paul E Pieris shows the pagoda, i.e. the devale, in the same place where the Visnu Devale is today. There is no evidence that a map of Devundara was prepared by the Portuguese before the date of the destruction of its shrines by them in 1587. In fact, the original which has been reproduced by Dr Pieris bears the date 1650, i.e. ten years after the Portuguese finally lost control of the districts around Devundara.

This map of Devundara must have been prepared after they had ceased to be masters of the place, for it also shows on the sea-coast a stockade. The Portuguese had no stockade there, but de Queyroz mentions that the Hollanders had one. The pagoda or devale shown must, therefore, have existed at Devundara at a date between the abandonment of the Matara District by the Portuguese and the date of its publication in Lisbon, i.e. 1650.

No devale was built at Devundara during the period of Portuguese occupation; but de Queyroz states that, after the King of Kandy gained control of the maritime districts, he lost no time in restoring the shrines which were destroyed by the Portuguese. The pagoda or devale at Devundara was one of the shrines so restored by Rajasimha II, King of Kandy.
Plate No. 25 of Dr Pieris's publication, quoted above, also contains a drawing of the elevation of the pagoda at Devundara. The architectural style does not seem to be in accordance with anything that existed before the advent of the Portuguese, but would be in keeping with that of Kandyan buildings. The map and plan published by Dr Pieris are, therefore, evidence of the existence of the Visnu Devale at Devundara in the seventeenth century at the self-same spot where it exists today.

When the Sinhalese regained control of the area, they no doubt destroyed the church which the Portuguese had built on the ruins of earlier shrines. The belief held by the Portuguese that their church stood on the site of Upulvan's shrine no doubt led the Sinhalese under Rajasimha II to build the Visnu Devale on the site which it occupies today.

H E Ameresekere quotes from an article in Vol. XI of the Journal of the Ceylon Branch of the Royal Asiatic Society (p 320) which describes the visit of Dutch sailor, surgeon and explorer Gautier Schouten to Dondra in 1661[2]:

> *At noon we reached the small town of Dondery* [Dondra]. *We found it bordered the sea and was inhabited by Cingalese. Some of them told us that in former times it had been one of the principal towns of the Kingdom of Candy, and they shewed us the remains and ruins of the ancient royal palace* [the main temple here was called Raja-gé]. *The ruined walls still bore witness to the beauty and great size which formerly had marked the buildings. We were told that since the war between the King of Kandy and the Portuguese, the power of the latter had worked this destruction. The broken down walls lay in heaps of debris. Overgrown with jungle, unsafe and full of hollows, where tigers, jackals, wolves, snakes and many other creatures found a hiding place.*

This creates a conflict with Paranavitana's views quoted above. If Schouten visited Dondra in 1661 and found the place in ruins with overgrown jungle and teeming with wild animals, the temple could not have been restored by 1650 as stated by Paranavitana. When Schouten returned to Europe, a book about his travels was published with the title *Voyage de Gautier Schouten aux Indes orientales, commence l'an 1658 et fini l'an 1665.* This means that the date of his visit to Dondra of 1661 is likely to be correct and in any case, lies between 1658 and 1665. The manuscript from which P E Pieris obtained the drawings for his book *Portuguese Maps and Plans of Ceylon, 1650,* has the title *Plantas das Fortalezas, Pagodes, & ca. da Ilha de Ceilao,* and Pieris has added a note that the volume bears the date 1650. This does not necessarily mean that the drawing of the front elevation of the Pagoda at Devinuwara was done in 1650, it was probably done some time before the Portuguese burnt it down in 1587.

Col. Colin McKenzie, later to become Surveyor General of India, visited Dondra in 1796 and wrote a detailed description of the place[3]:

> *After a short view, we were conducted from thence to the sea-beach of Dewunder-head* [Dondra-head] , *scarcely 1400 yards distant, by a gradual descent along a walk or avenue in*

the woods; in walking over this ground, several remains of ancient buildings resembling the Carnatick [South Indian] *temples struck us forcibly, and induced as narrow an inspection as could be made in a couple of hours.*

Close to the beach we find the first avenue or building, probably designed for the use of devotees immediately before or after ablution in the sea, which is not forty yards off; the descent over the bank is not difficult, though the coast is lined with masses of granite washed by the waves. It consists of a colonnade of sixteen pillars of granite about nine feet high, the four centre ones of which only are cut to regular forms with bases and capitals: it exactly fronts the line of the avenue to the temple on the height: on its north side are two pillars also sculptured, forming an exact square with the two central ones of the colonnade, in the centre of which is a square opening of about two and a half feet on the sides faced with stone but nearly filled up with earth; this seems to have been the situation of the interior recess where the object of worship was placed of which and of the roof no vestige remains. [This is definitely a reference to the Simhasana where Skanda rested, shown previously in Figs. 5 and 6.]

Proceeding thence by an early ascent, we cross the ruins of a wall probably the enclosure of the grand temple, marked by several pillars and upright stones, but no sculptures are to be seen till we reach the Cingalese temple, nearly fronting which stands the inner portal of a Hindu temple, consisting of two upright stones supporting a cross one, all carved on one face, with ornaments similar to the interior parts of the pagodas on the coast, the centre of the cross stone occupied by a fierce fantastic head, the sides by a running border of foliage, and the basement supported by figures exactly in the same style and taste. [This is a reference to the Gateway previously shown in Fig. 13.]

To the left of the Cingalese building are more ruins, evidently the remains of other temples: the steps leading up to the raised floors of these are decorated with the heads of elephants, carved of stones placed on either side; an ornament frequently to be observed in Hindu temples, as entrances of Egyptian buildings were ornamented with those of the sphynx.

Near these we meet a deep well, across the mouth of which was placed a flat granite stone, with a perforation six inches square through its centre, between the figure of the prints of two feet raised on the stone; the figure occupying the rest of the stone is scooped out to the depth of two feet. It is probable that the well was included within some of the buildings now no longer existing; its use does not appear; the cross stone was too heavy to be easily moved, and occupies too much room to admit of water being drawn from it for any common use; the figures carved on it indicate some connection with the Lingam and the Phallus; and may furnish a key to the object of worship here.

On narrowly examining these remains, little doubt remained in my mind that this was the site of an ancient Hindu temple, on the ruins of which the Cingalese building was raised at a much later period. The revolutions of religion, in which the first was overturned and almost every vestige of worship destroyed, to make room for the other, would, probably be explained by the Cingalese history, an abstract of which is published in Valentyn's book, under the article Ceylon.

The name of the place Divi-n-oor-Dewalla favours the opinion, and when we recollect the partiality of the Hindus to build their religious structures in places near the sea, to water, to the spring heads of rivers, on the tops of remarkable hills, and mountains and situations favourable to retirement from the world, and to purer ablutions, according to their ideas; in places to which the extraordinary length and toil of the journey attached a superior degree of merit; as instanced in the pilgrimages to Jagarrat[4] *and Ramifur*[5] *; to the wilds of Purwuttum*[6] *; to Tripetty*[7] *; to the sources of the Godavery*[8] *at Trimbuck Nasser*[9] *, and of the Kistna*[10] *at Balifur*[11]*; we need not be surprised to find a fane of Mahadeo*[12] [Siva] *reared on the utmost bounds of Lankadeep, and their habitable world; and shall be ready to suppose that the ablutions at the furthest point of Ramifur*[13] *become the greatest extent of their pilgrimages only, when revolutions, of which we have no distinct accounts, and the introduction of a foreign religion* *and nation into Ceylon, rendered pilgrimage to Devinoor* [Thondeswaram] *no longer practicable.*

Regarding the last three lines of the above quotation, a similar 'revolution' occurred here in the 1980s. Prof J C Holt records an interview with the Chief Kapurala of the Devinuwara Vishnu Devalaya, who told him that[14]:

He also said that before the ethnic conflict arose in the early 1980s, a significant number of Tamil devotees from South India or the northern Jaffna Peninsula of the island would frequent the devalaya, but they had now stopped visiting almost completely.

Eudelin de Jonville (1756-1837) was a French Cartographer who was employed by the first British Governor, Frederick North. He was appointed Surveyor General and also acted as the Superintendent of the Botanical and Cinnamon Gardens. He travelled around Ceylon and wrote a *Journal of a Tour in the Galle and Matara Districtsin 1800.* He visited Dondra in 1800 and mentions seeing a two and a half foot long Lingam lying on the ground, but unfortunately does not state the exact location where he saw this Lingam[15]:

On the way, I stopped at the pagoda of Deoundere [Dondra] , *set on the most southerly point of the island. This pagoda is dedicated to Vishnou, and was built by Daboulouessen Ragia* [King Dapulusen] *in 1332 of the Boudhou era, 789 AD. What little remains of the ancient edifice clearly shows its plan, a long rectangle, to which corresponds a gallery of three or four hundred pillars. The new temple is insignificant. Among the debris on the ground is a lingam, two and a half feet long, which the priest of the place called 'Isvara roupe'. 'Figure of Isvara'.*

Captain Robert Percival (1765-1826) of His Majesty's Eighteenth or Royal Irish Regiment visited Dondra before 1803. His description of the place is very similar to that of Col. Colin McKenzie who visited the place a few years earlier. He too arrived at the conclusion that the ruins adjacent to the Vishnu Devalaya are that of a Hindu temple[16]:

About half a mile from this temple is the point of Dondre Head, to which you proceed along an avenue, where there are ruins of several more temples resembling those on the Coromandel coast. Close to the coast is a building designed for the use of devotees who perform their last ablution in the sea. The descent though great is not difficult. The shore below is lined with rocks of granite washed by the waves. This building is encircled by rows of pillars of granite about ten feet high. Between the pillars and the main body of this temple are little square compartments, where the devotees sit to refresh themselves.

Beyond this is the inner portal of a Hindu temple, consisting of two upright stones, supporting s cross one, all covered on one side with ornaments similar to those on the Coromandel coast. To the left are the ruins of more temples; the steps and slabs of stone discovered here and there are almost buried by the earth. Those leading up to platforms or raised floors are decorated with figures of elephants' heads and other beasts, and of men and women naked.

Near this spot is a deep well, the mouth covered with a black granite, with a hole through its centre. Two prints of a foot are seen on this stone, and a figure is scooped out two feet in depth. This well has every appearance of having been enclosed in some building now not existing, nor is the use of the top stone ever properly explained to the visitors. It is too heavy to be easily moved. On narrowly investigating these remains of antiquity, and comparing them with the religion and works made in the present and last centuries by the Ceylonese, they do not appear to belong originally to the present inhabitants of Ceylon, but altogether correspond with the opinions and workmanship of the Hindoos. Cingalese temples seem to have been erected at a much later period on the sites of those originally constructed by the Hindoos

Fig. 22: Cordiner's reproduction of a drawing of Vishnu and Skanda from the Vishnu Devale, 1800.

Rev. James Cordiner was Chaplain to the Garrison of Colombo and also Principal of all the schools in Colombo from 1799 to 1804. He travelled widely in Ceylon and visited Dondra in 1800. He published a book about Ceylon in 1807. An illustration of an image from the Vishnu Devale which is in his book is reproduced as Fig. 22. In his description of Dondra he mentions seeing 'the poor remains of a Hindu temple', a Lingam being revered, a Vishnu Devale, another Vishnu temple presumably Hindu, and a stone image of Ganesa[17]:

> *On a flat green, five hundred yards from the extremity of Dondra, stands the poor remains of a Hindoo temple, probably once the most magnificent structure in the island of Ceylon. About two hundred stone pillars, some neatly cut with bases and capitals, others as rough as they came from the quarry, are still seen in an erect position. A long avenue of those stretches directly towards the sea, intersected by other rows leading to the right and left. About the centre of them stands the stone frame of a door, consisting of two square pillars supporting a lintel, carved on one face, in a style similar to the inner portals of other Hindoo pagodas, exhibiting heads of stern aspect, and borders of running foliage.*

There are likewise shattered relics of several images strewed among the ruins: one of these is of the head of an elephant of the size of life, not badly sculptured. Here is a deep well covered by a flat stone containing a square aperture, with a carved impression of a foot on each side of it: this place was constructed for the sake of cleanliness, at a time when the pagoda was frequented by multitudes of people. Near it stands a Lingam, or altar to Mahadeo [Siva] *in his generative character, having a canopy of leaves erected over it, apparently still frequented and revered.*

Close to this is now raised a temple of Buddha distinguished by the title of Devinura Maha Visnu Dewaley, similar to that of Agraboddhagama but of smaller size. Adjoining to it stands a humble sanctuary, built of mud but with a thatched roof, dedicated to Vishnu. It is divided into several apartments, hung round with printed calico exhibiting various imaginary deities.

Amongst these is Carticeya [Skanda], *the titular god of Cattergam* [Kataragama], *a celebrated pagoda, at no great distance, within the territories of the King of Candy. This is a human figure with six heads, and twelve arms, riding sideways on a peacock holding a live serpent in its mouth. Before it stands a table and a basin, where the worshippers present their offerings. At the same place is an ancient stone image of Ganesa, in miniature, having the head of an elephant with the body of a man.*

Major Jonathan Forbes of the 78th Highlanders visited Dondra in the 1830s and included a description of Dondra in a book that he published. He mentions a single pillar and remains of an ancient building, over which the sea breaks[18]:

Dondera, or Dewinuwara (city of god), is situated four miles from Matura, on a narrow peninsula, the most southerly point of Ceylon, latitude 5° 50" N. and longitude 80° 40" E. Here, interspersed among the native huts, gardens, and cocoa-nut plantations, several hundred upright stone pillars still remain: they are cut into various shapes, and exhibit *different sculptures; amongst others, Rama, with his bow and arrows, may be discerned in various forms.*

A square gateway, formed of three stones elaborately carved, leads to a wretched 'mud edifice', in which four stone windows of superior workmanship are evidences that a very different style of building had formerly occupied this hovel. It is now, however, the only temple of Vishnu at Dewinuwara; a station reckoned particularly sacred by his votaries, as being the utmost limit which now remains of his conquests when incarnate in that perfect prince and peerless warrior, Ramachandra.

Although his temple is so mean, the place retains much of its sanctity; and an annual festival, which takes place at the full moon in the month of July, continues to attract many thousands of the worshippers of Vishnu. From the temple, a broad road, overshadowed by cocoa-nut trees, leads to a group of plain stone pillars near the sea-shore; but from these my attention was attracted by a single pillar, situated on a low rocky point, over which the sea breaks amidst hewn stones, the remains of some ancient building.

If Rama's expedition and conquest of Lanka existed in any form, or had any foundation more material than a poet's fancy, this lone pillar may be considered as an index that has resisted the waste of ages, and now battles with the waves of ocean to maintain its position, and mark the utmost limit which remains of Vishnu's conquests and religion. The pillar is of a form alternately octagonal and square, and exactly resembles columns that are to be seen on the sacred promontory of Trinkomalee.

Charles Pridham wrote a comprehensive book published in 1849 about Ceylon titled *An Historical, Political and Statistical Account of Ceylon and its Dependencies.* He visited Dondra and his description is similar to that of Major Forbes quoted immediately above. He also mentions the lone pillar 'Near the seashore is a group of plain stone pillars, and on a low rocky point a single pillar, over which the sea breaks amidst hewn stones, the remains of some ancient building[19]'. Elsewhere in his book he quotes numerous references to ancient annals which record the steady encroachment of the sea into the island steadily reducing its size.

Sir James Emerson Tennent was Colonial Secretary of Ceylon from 1845 to 1850. After his return to UK he wrote a comprehensive book about Ceylon in two volumes. He had visited Dondra and gave a detailed description in his book[20]:

> *Dondera Head, the Sunium* [southernmost point] *of Ceylon, and the southern extremity of the island, is covered with the ruins of a temple, which was once the most celebrated in Ceylon. The headland itself has been the resort of devotees and pilgrims, from the most remote ages;- Ptolemy describes it as Dagana, "sacred to the moon", and the Buddhists constructed there one of their earliest dagobas, the restoration of which was the care of successive sovereigns.*
> *But the most important temple was a shrine which in very early times had been erected by the Hindus in honour of Vishnu. It was in the height of splendour, when, in 1587, the place was devastated in the course of the marauding expedition by which De Souza d'Arronches sought to create a diversion, during the siege of Colombo by Raja Singha II. The historians of the period state that at that time Dondera was the most renowned place of pilgrimage in Ceylon; Adam's Peak scarcely excepted.*
>
> *The temple, they say, was so vast, that from the sea it had the appearance of a city. The pagoda was raised on vaulted arches, richly decorated, and roofed with plates of gilded copper. It was encompassed by a quadrangular cloister, opening under verandahs, upon a terrace and gardens with odoriferous shrubs and trees, whose flowers were gathered by the priests for processions.*
>
> *De Souza entered the gates without resistance; and his soldiers tore down the statues, which were more than a thousand in number. The temples and its buildings were overthrown, its arches and its colonnades were demolished, and its gates and towers levelled with the ground. The plunder was immense, in ivory, gems, jewels, sandalwood and ornaments of gold. As the last indignity that could be offered to the sacred place, cows were slaughtered in the*

courts, and the cars of the idols, with other combustible materials, being fired, the shrine was reduced to ashes.

A stone doorway, exquisitely carved, and a small building, whose extraordinary strength resisted the violence of the destroyers, are all that now remain standing; but the ground for a considerable distance is strewn with ruins, conspicuous among which are numbers of finely cut columns of granite. The dagoba which stood on the crown of a hill, is a mound of shapeless debris.

Captain Horatio J Suckling of the Ceylon Rifles wrote a book about Ceylon in 1876, but he did not give his name as the author. In the book, he describes Ibn Battuta's visit to Ceylon. He says that Ibn Battuta was carried to the top of Adams Peak in a palanquin with sixteen bearers, in relays, presumably. He repeats Ibn Battuta's description of Devinuwara given earlier and then goes on to say[21]:

Ptolemy's Dagana luna sacra, hence the Arabian Agna Dana Dinewar, and the modern Dondra, appears to have been always a place of importance and resort of pilgrims. It is doubtful if it ever was a Buddhist place of worship, even now pilgrims to Ramiseram [Rameswaram] *pass on to the temple of Dondra, which is dedicated to Sewa* [Siva]. *The great building of which Ibn Battuta speaks was sacked and destroyed by Souza de Aronches, in 1587. It was covered with plates of gilded brass, and contained 1000 statues. The ruins of the ancient temple still encumber the ground, among which are many finely cut granite pillars and carved stones.*

Constance Fredrica Gordon Cumming (1837-1924) was a travel writer who spent her life travelling around the world and writing many travel books. She spent two years in Ceylon about 1890 and wrote a book about Ceylon. She visited Dondra and describes the annual Esala Perahera which is held in July/August. It is the oldest Perahera in the country by far and has been held for over 750 years. Her description is as follows[22]:

Now this ancient relic-shrine is likewise a ruin, and the modern worshippers of Buddha, Vishnu and Siva make common cause, the shrines of the Hindoo deities flanking those of Buddha and his disciples in the Buddhist temple. Once a year, at the time of the midsummer full moon, this quiet village is the scene of a great religious festival and fair, combined attractions which attract thousands of pilgrims and other folks to Dondra Head for a week's holiday; and very picturesque these crowds must be, all in their gayest attire, camped beneath the palms and along the shore.

Rows of temporary sheds are erected and rapidly transformed into hundreds of small shops for the sale of all manner of food, fruit, cakes, curry-stuffs, confectionary, native books, Tangalla brass-ware, tortoise shell combs, tobacco leaves, betel leaves and arecanuts, cloth, cheap jewellery and toys.

The religious ceremony is a Perahera, when the shrine containing some precious relic is carried round the village in solemn procession, followed by lay and ecclesiastical officials in their Kandyan state dress, and escorted by a troupe of trumpeters, shell-blowers, and tom-tom beaters, making their usual deafening noise.

Edward Russell Ayrton (1882-1914) started his archaeological career as an Egyptologist. Working for Theodore M Davis in Egypt's Valley of the Kings they discovered in 1905/8 the tombs of the Pharoahs Siptah and Horemheb. In 1911 he accepted the position of Archaeological Commissioner of Ceylon. He was the second person to hold this post after the pioneer, H C P Bell. In March 1914 he visited Dondra and spent several days there. He made copious diary notes during his visit intending to write an article later. Alas this was not to be, he died two months later during a hunting expedition, accidentally drowned in the Tissamaharama Tank. He was only 32 years old. Some selected extracts from his diary notes of March 1914 are given below[23]. Ayrton interprets 'Nagarisa Nila Temple' as Vishnu Temple but as Paranavitana has pointed out, this arises from a wrong reading of an inscription by Rhys Davids as mentioned earlier where he read 'nam' as 'nila'. Nam means named. Therefore it should be Nagarisa Nam Temple i.e. a Temple of Siva[24].

The ruins at Dondra

13 March 1914: Went over to Dondra, and down to see the two small Kovils on the sea shore.

Of these, one on the rocks, said by the Kapurala to be the place where the Kataragam Deviyo landed, is marked by only one standing and three fallen pillars.

The other Kovil [see Fig. 5] *is at the coast end of the road leading due south from the great gate of the Vishnu Devale. It is a group of pillars of which all except the two of the entrance and the four of the shrine are mere rough blocks of stone and therefore probably originally in a wall. The four of the shrine are now connected by coral and mud wall and the room has a thatched kadjan roof. In the room there is an altar slab (in pieces) of granite placed wrong side up on a coral and mud base. Originally it must have stood on a pillar as the hollow in the bottom indicates.*

The Kapurala said that offerings are made here to Kattragam Deviyo, and that he sat on this stone after landing. Being pressed the Kapurala owned that the stone had been found lying in fragments nearby and was set up here recently. The Devale is now called the Devundara Singhasana.

In the introduction to the Dondra Vihare's Visitors Book it is stated that the Temple of Galturu-mulpaya or modern Parama-wichitrarama Vihare with three shrines, pagoda, with relics of Buddha, Bo tree and two consecrated edifices stood in the heart of the town of Dondra. Galturu-mulpaya was originally a four storied building. It possessed Devales. The old name of the town was Devanagara and does not mean the City of Gods but the "City of the King of Gods – Vishnu". This appears to have been the original temple here – that of Vishnu, the Buddhist shrines being a later addition. The Situ Pilimage is old though later than the Vishnu temple, but all the present Dagaba and pansalas are more modern, being built at a higher level and with the old materials.

> *It is traditional that at that time there were* [here] *18 Maha Veethi (large roads), 18 ordinary roads, 18 Obukku (broad roads), 18 Mudukku (paths or lanes), 18 Thonadi (wells), 18 vewu (tanks); at the four cardinal points there were four Devales.*
>
> *Approximately half mile to the south is Kandaswami's Kovil. Tradition that he landed there on a stone patuwa (raft), where the fallen stone pillars are on a cluster of rocks at the sea beach, and then settled at the place above, due south from the south entrance of the Maluwa of the Temple.*
>
> *The Ganesa* [Fig. 17] *and Nandi* [Fig. 7] *at the Pansala are said to have been found near the light-house, but there are no remains* [here] *now.*
>
> *The Devales are the eastern part and at present consist of a large Vishnu Devale – built in the shrine of the old temple – of whitewashed brick or stone, thatched with (?tiles) cadjans. Facing the south is standing stucco figure of Vishnu. The walls are decorated with his Avatars.*
>
> *The tradition is that there was a stone image of Vishnu here which looked straight out to sea. All shipping was at a standstill since ships could not pass his glance until a man named 'Goldsmith' made it look down. This image, says tradition, was removed to Alutnuwara when the temple fell into ruin and then to Dambulla.*

R L Brohier (1892-1980) joined the Survey Department as a Surveyor and rose to the position of Deputy Surveyor General. He wrote several books but his magnum opus was a three volume *Ancient Irrigation Works in Ceylon* which was first published in 1934. He also wrote a travel book about Ceylon in which one chapter was titled *Dondra – City of the Gods.* In it he says[25]:

> *In no other part of the Island perhaps is the early place of Hinduism so plainly traceable through the later Buddhist tradition.*

He continues with a detailed description of the annual Perahera in Dondra and ends the chapter with the following words[26]:

> *This explains why the magic of Dondra lies today in words, just words with wonderful associations, and nothing much else to show for the hold it has retained on national sentiment. That is why, once a year by the holding of a festival, the City of Gods squeezes out romantic poetry from the melancholy which has overtaken ancient glory.*

Notes:

1. **Paranavitana S,** 1953, The Shrine of Upulvan at Devundara, *Memoirs of the Archaeological Survey of Ceylon, Volume VI,* Colombo, pp 16-17.
2. **Ameresekere H E**, (1931), Vimal Sri Dewunuwara, *Ceylon Literary Register, Third Series, Vol. I, 1931,* p 279.
3. **McKenzie, Capt. C,** Remarks on some Antiquities on the West and South Coasts of Ceylon; written in the year 1796, *Asiatic Researches, Volume VI,* London, 1801, pp 425-454.
4. Probably Jagannath of Puri, Orissa, a holy Vishnu sea-side temple. The size of the huge chariot (*theyr*) in which the deity is taken round the streets during festivals gave rise to the English word 'juggernaut'.
5. Probably Rameswaram near Dhanuskodi, opposite Talaimannar, the site of one of the holiest Sivan temples in India and one of the twelve Jyotirlingams of India.
6. A reference to the Srisailum Sivan temple on the banks of the River Krishna in Andhra Pradesh, one of the twelve Jyotirlingams. It was visited by Colin McKenzie in 1794.
7. Tirupati in Andhra Pradesh, one of the holiest Hindu pilgrimage sites in India. It has a Venkateshwara temple.
8. The River Godaveri in India is the second longest river there after the River Ganges.
9. Triambakeshwar – the source of the River Godaveri.
10. The River Krishna is the fourth biggest river in India.
11. Probably a reference to Maha-Baleshwar, the source of the River Krishna.
12. Another name for Siva.
13. Rameswaram, see Note 5 above.
14. **Holt J C,** 2004, *The Buddhist Visnu: Religious Transformation, Politics, and Culture,* New York, p 355.

15. **Raven-Hart, Major R**, 1963, *Travels in Ceylon 1700 – 1800,* translated and edited by Major R Raven-Hart, Colombo, p 87.
16. **Percival, Captain R**, 1803, *An Account of the Island of Ceylon,* reprinted by Tisara Prakasakayo Ltd., Dehiwala, 1975, p 101-102.
17. **Cordiner, Rev. J**, 1807, *A Description of Ceylon, Vol. I,* London, pp 195-197.
18. **Forbes, Major J**, 1841, *Eleven years in Ceylon, Vol. 2,* 2nd edition, London, pp 176-179.
19. **Ameresekere**, 1931, pp 282-283.
20. **Tennent, Sir J E**, 1859, *Ceylon, Physical, Historical and Topographical,* London, in two volumes, 3rd ed., Vol. 2, Part VII, Chap. 1, pp 113-114.
21. **An Officer, late of the Ceylon Rifles**, 1876, *Ceylon: A general description of the Island, Historical, Physical, Statistical,* London. Pp 261-262. The author is believed to be Capt. Horatio J Suckling.
22. **Gordon Cumming, C F**, 1893, *Two Happy Years in Ceylon,* London, p 447.
23. **Ayrton, E R**, Antiquities in the Southern Province, Diary of the late Mr E R Ayrton, Archaeological Commissioner of Ceylon, with notes by John M Senaveratna, *Ceylon Antiquary and Literary Register, Vol VI, Part 3, pp 151-152, January 1921, and Part 4, pp 191-197, April 1921.*
24. **Paranavitana S,** pp 13 and 75.
25. **Brohier, R L**, 1965, *Seeing Ceylon: In vistas of Scenery, History, legend and Folklore,* Colombo, p 159.
26. Ibid, p 163.

9
THONDESWARAM SIVAN TEMPLE
Where was it?

Vijaya founded a temple to Lord Santhirasegaram (he who wears the crescent on the crown) at Dondra Head, though later we hear nothing about it in the Ceylon chronicles ... Unfortunately, these sacred abodes of the gods, after being robbed of their wealth, were razed to the ground by the Portuguese. In the course of time the Vishnu Devale was rebuilt, but not the Saivite shrine Nagarisa[1].

It has been established that there was a Sivan Temple in Devinuwara. The Siva Lingam and the Nandhi which are present are incontrovertible proof. The question then arises, where precisely was the Thondeswaram of Pancheswaram located? According to the evidence that has been presented, there are three possible locations, and each one will be considered in turn.

(1) In the Galgé (Stone Temple) in the outskirts of the town.

(2) In the Main Temple Complex area

(3) Near the sea beach, in Kovil Watta, near the Lighthouse, or in a location now engulfed by the advancing sea.

In Chapter 1, a quotation from the London weekly Journal, *Newslanka* of 05 November 1998 mentioned the discovery of a Siva Lingam buried shallowly in front of the Othpilima Vihara in the main temple complex. The quotation also says that "*At an earlier occasion too a similar sculpture was found at the same premises*". If that statement is correct, it immediately raises the possibility that there was more than one Temple of Siva.

I
Temple of Siva in the Galgé

The Galgé is in the classical Dravidian style of temple architecture of the Pallava period. Paranavitana has assigned it a date of seventh century AD. This makes it by far the oldest existing stone temple in Lanka. Even in India, stone temple construction started only at about this time. He describes the quiet dignity of it as follows[2]:

> *There are no sculptural ornamentations on the exterior of the building, and those on the doorway hardly attract one's attention. The designers of the shrine, therefore, relied on the form of the building itself, and not on any adventitious decorative designs, in order to impress the votaries. This marked restraint shown in the application of ornament, and its harmonious and balanced proportions, impart to this small shrine a quiet dignity lacking in more pretentious edifices raised with much greater labour.*

Paranavithana goes on to say[3]:

> *Free standing edifices of any importance, constructed entirely or mainly of stone, so far known in the island, are those dating from periods of Tamil rule, for instance, Saiva shrines at Polonnaruva, or – when they had been raised at the command of Sinhalese rulers – due to inspiration from South India, as is the case with the shrine at Gadaladeniya, They thus represent phases in the evolution of Dravidian architecture, and not that of the Sinhalese.*

As regards the vimanam or spire above the inner chamber, it must have existed originally as there are traces of a few layers of construction even today. There is also the evidence that the inner chamber has much thicker walls and roof than the outer chamber, and therefore had to carry much more weight above it. Paranavitana says that[4]:

> *The method adopted for the roofing of the garbha-grha, differing as it does from that of the ante-chamber, indicates*

that this roof required additional strength to carry a weight which the roof over the ante-chamber had not to bear. It is likely, therefore, that originally there was a sikhara marking the sanctum, and that the ante-chamber had a flat roof.

E R Ayrton, the Archaeological Commissioner visited Dondra in 1914. He wrote some diary notes about his visit which included a paragraph about Galgé. He is convinced that there was a spire (Vimanam) above the roof of the building which has now disappeared[5]:

On the hill behind the village of Dondra is the Gal-gé. A small Vishnu (?) Devale in good condition; had this cleared of roots and jungle. Owing to the wall being double with rubble between, roots growing in the rubble have forced off the outer face on the west side. The brick spire has completely disappeared. The doorways slant.

The cover of this book is an artist's impression of what the Galgé would have originally looked like when it was first built with the vimanam.

The area surrounding the temple has been levelled off to a considerable extent. This indicates that the stone structure is a central portion for the main deity and that it would have been surrounded by other structures made of wood or brick, of which no traces now remain.

Unfortunately, there is nothing to give a clue as to the deity that was in the temple. Paranavitana comments[6]:

Whatever cult object was in the garbha-grha, it had disappeared long ago, and there is no evidence in or about the shrine giving a clue to the identity of the faith to which this fane was dedicated ... The Galgé bears no writing on the walls, nor has any inscription been found in its vicinity, that would throw light on its identity and purpose or the date of its original foundation.

Col. Colin McKenzie, later to become Surveyor General of India, visited the site in 1796 and had no doubts about the deity that was originally installed here, believing it to be a Siva Lingam[7]:

> *Though the figure of the* [Siva] *Lingam, cow* [Nandhi], *and every object of Hindu veneration, seems purposely removed, enough remains, in the simplicity of the style of the architecture and its few decorations, to ascertain its claims to antiquity; and this shews the use of classing the objects of this kind we frequently meet dispersed over India.*

The official website of the Devinuwara Temple also said that it was a Temple of Siva[8]:

> *This* [Vishnu] *devale is said to be situated at the spot where king Rawana had fallen dead and the place where the present galgé is said to be the spot where prince Rama took aim to shoot Rawana. This was a temple for god Shiwa* [Siva].

As Paranavitana points out, in the *Paravi Sandesa* the bird spends the day viewing the sites of the city and at dusk proceeds to the *Raja-gé* to watch the ritual dances. This principal shrine at Devinuwara is also described in the *Kokila Sandesa* as the *Raja -gé,* and he goes on to explain what this term means[9]:

> *It is referred to as raja-gé (King's House), and it must have occupied the same position in the city as did a palace at a royal seat. The term raja-gé corresponds to the Tamil kovil or koyil and, as in a Hindu kovil, the ritual must have been modelled on the daily routine of a king in a royal palace. The dance of the young women in the evening, conducted daily at the shrine, which from the poet's description differed in no way from that described as having been a feature of Prince Sapumal's court at Jaffna, is evidence to this effect.*

This implies that the principal shrine at Devinuwara was a Hindu Kovil, and could well have been the Galgé.

II
Temple of Siva in the Main Temple complex area

The second possibility is that the Temple of Siva was in the main Temple complex area where the Buddhist Vihara, Dagaba, and Vishnu Devale are located. The Siva Lingam was found in this area in front of the Othpilima Vihara in 1998. If the *Newslanka* report of this finding is correct, this was the second Siva Lingam found in this area (See Chapter I). The Nandhi (Bull and Siva's gate-guardian) is also in the courtyard here, but there is a belief that the Nandhi was found in an area near the beach and brought up here a long time ago. Nevertheless, the discovery of a Lingam and a Nandhi in this area does point to the possibility of the Temple of Siva having been somewhere here.

There is also the evidence of the Lamp Pillar described in Chapter 2. Paranavitana identifies the figure on one face as that of Siva drawing a bow called Pinaka[10].This adds circumstantial evidence to there being a Temple of Siva in the vicinity, but if so, where could it have been located. There are still several hundred stone pillars in this area. Could these have been part of a Sivan Temple?

In Chapter 8, several visitors to Dondra have mentioned the ruins of Hindu temples in the main temple complex area. To recapitulate them:

(1) Colin McKenzie visited Dondra in 1796 and wrote that to the left of the Vishnu Devale

> "*are more ruins, evidently the ruins of more temples: the steps leading to the raised floors are decorated with the heads of elephants, carved of stones placed on either side, an ornament frequently to be observed in Hindu temples ...*
>
> *... the figures carved on it* [over a well] *indicate some connection with the Lingam and Phallus, and may furnish a key to the object of worship here.*
>
> *On narrowly examining these remains, little doubt remained in my mind that this was the site of an ancient Hindu temple, on the ruins of which the Cingalese building was raised at a much later period*".

(2) Eudelin de Jonville visited Dondra in 1800 and wrote

"*Among the debris on the ground is a Lingam, two and a half feet long, which the priest called 'Isvara roupe', 'Figure of Isvara'.* Unfortunately, Jonville did not say where exactly in the main temple complex this Lingam was lying.

(3) Captain Robert Percival visited Dondra just before 1803 and wrote

"*To the left* [of the stone gateway] *are ruins of more temples" ... "On narrowly investigating these remains of antiquity, and comparing them with the religion and works made in the present and last centuries by the Ceylonese, they do not appear to belong to the present inhabitants of Ceylon, but altogether correspond with the opinions and workmanship of the Hindoos. Cingalese temples seem to have been erected at a much later period on the sites of those originally constructed by the Hindoos'.*

(4) Rev. James Cordiner visited Dondra in 1800 and wrote

"On a flat green, five hundred yards from the extremity of Dondra, stands the poor remains of a Hindoo temple, probably one of the most magnificent structures in the island of Ceylon ...

... near it [a well] *stands a Lingam, or altar to the Mahadeo* [Siva] *in his generative character, having a canopy of leaves erected over it, apparently still frequented and revered".*

(5) Captain Horatio J Suckling visited Dondra just before 1876 and wrote

"*It is doubtful if it ever was a Buddhist place of worship, even now pilgrims to Ramiseram* [Rameswaram] *pass on to the temple of Dondra, which is dedicated to Sewa* [Siva].

The consensus of opinion seems to be that to the left of the Vishnu Devale there was a Temple of Siva.

III
On or near the sea beach

The third possible location for the Sivan temple is near the sea beach, in the area known as Kovil Watta, near the Lighthouse (see Fig. 23), or in a location now engulfed by the advancing sea. There is a belief that the Nandi and Ganesa statue now in the main temple complex were originally in the area known as Kovil Watta. Although there are no ruins here, the fact that the area is still known as 'Kovil Watta' indicates that some time in the past there were Hindu temples here. If they were Buddhist temples, the area would have been known as 'Devale Watta'.

Fig. 23 Dondra Lighthouse
(Courtesy - Sri Lanka Ports Authority)

The *Paravi Sandesa* written in the fifteenth century by the famous Sri Rahula establishes beyond doubt that the Ganesa temple was near the sea-shore[11]:

> ... *the bird* [a dove] *was asked to spend the night at a rest-house named Valle-madama (the Beach Hospice) which adjoined a shrine dedicated to Ganesa. We are further told that this Ganesa temple was built in the name of the 'well known Rama-candra', a merchant prince. His name and his devotion to Ganesa proclaim him to have hailed from India, probably from the Tamil country. At dawn, the bird would be awakened by the music for the morning service at the Ganesa shrine ...*

> *... The references in these poems establish that there were, in the fourteenth and fifteenth centuries, three distinct groups of sanctuaries at Devundara. The Ganesa shrine and possibly other Saiva places of worship existed on the beach.*

The last sentence above indicates the possibility of a Sivan temple also on the beach. When the Ganesa and Nandhi stone statues that were near the beach were transported to the main temple complex a long time ago, the Siva Lingam could also have been transported along with them.

Fig. 24: Rocky sea shore at Dondra Head (Photo - Thiru Arumugam)

Another possibility is that the solitary pillar standing in the rocks in the sea is a marker of the place where the temple of Siva was located. There are three references to this pillar. The rocky shore can be seen in Fig. 24. Major Forbes who visited Dondra in the 1830s says[12]:

... but from these my attention was attracted by a single pillar, situated on a low rocky point, over which the sea breaks amidst hewn stones, the remains of some ancient building. If Rama's expedition and conquest of Lanka existed in any form, or had any foundation more material than a poet's fancy, this lone pillar may be considered as an index which has resisted the waste of ages, and now battles with the waves of ocean to maintain its position ...

Charles Pridham who visited Dondra in the 1840s also mentions this pillar[13]:

Near the sea shore is a group of stone pillars, and on a low rocky point a single pillar, over which the sea breaks over hewn stones, the remains of some ancient building ...

Archaeological Commissioner Ayrton mentions this twice in his Dondra field visit notes. He specifically says that the solitary pillar on the rocks is the site of a Kovil and that there are three more pillars in the water[14]:

13 March 1914: Went over at Dondra, and down to see the two small Kovils on the sea shore. Of these, one on the rocks, said by the Kapurala to be the place where the Katargam Deviyo landed, is marked by only one standing and three fallen pillars.

Tradition that he landed there on a stone patuwa (raft), where the fallen stone pillars are on a cluster of rocks at the sea beach ...

It is seen from inscription No. 6 in Chapter 6, that the Civil Servant Rhys Davids discovered in 1870 this stone slab inscription on the Dondra beach being washed by the waves. The inscription, dated about 1515, records the names and extant of lands which were the property of a shrine named Nagarisa-kovil. We have seen that this is a reference to a Temple of Siva. The inscription states that Vendarasa-konda-perumal, the Captain of the (King's) Bodyguard, bought and settled these properties so that offerings and observances to the god (Siva) may be maintained without cessation ... This is absolutely clear-cut evidence that there was a Temple of Siva nearby.

When the writer was walking along the Dondra beach at low tide, he came across a rock lying on the beach with an unusual feature. See Fig. 25. In the days before dynamite, the method of cracking rocks to obtain pieces of rock to sculpt was to make a series of deep holes along the line along which the rock needed to be broken, then fill the holes with glowing embers. The heating of the rock and resulting expansion, caused it to crack along the line of holes. From the photo it can be seen that the stone-mason has started making his series of holes, but for some unknown reason he has abandoned his task halfway. From the 'L' shaped piece of rock that he wanted to break off, it would appear that he wanted a piece of rock to carve a deity. One more piece of evidence that there was a temple nearby.

Fig. 25: Rock on beach at Dondra Head (Photo - Thiru Arumugam)

If indeed there was a temple here on the seashore in 1515 (the date of the inscription mentioned above) it would have been a sitting duck for the Portuguese marauding mission which arrived seven decades later. The canons mounted on their ships would have reduced the temple to rubble when fired upon at virtually point-blank range.

There is a final possibility for the location of the Temple of Siva, and that is that it was in a location which is now under the sea. The sea may have advanced in the normal process of sea erosion or there may have been a tsunami in the dim distant past. Local legends believe that Ravana's main palace, he had many palaces, was somewhere near the Dondra Lighthouse. Professor Anuradha Seneviratne has this comment[15]:

> *The rocks on which the light-house stands today in the Devundara sea-coast is believed to be the place where Ravana had his city of Lankapura and his palace and fortress. People call it Ravana Kotte. They say that the mighty waters of the ocean rushed over the capital by the act of gods to punish impious Ravana who held captive the wife of Rama. They buried twenty-five palaces and five hundred thousand streets.*

Ravana was a great scholar and author of books on astrology as well as on medical matters. He was a maestro of the South Indian stringed instrument, the veena. He was a Brahmin and an ardent worshipper of Siva. He is supposed to have carried a small gold Lingam with him at all times. It is therefore highly likely that he would have built a Temple for Siva near his palace in Dondra.

The travel writer, Constance F Gordon Cumming who visited Dondra about 1890 had these comments to make in her book about Ceylon[16]:

> *It was in this city* [Dondra] *that Ravana, the mighty king of the Isle, was besieged by Rama, a warrior prince of Oude, whose beautiful wife, Sita, had been carried off by Ravana, in revenge for insults offered to his sister. This city of palaces had seven fortified walls, and many towers and battlements of brass. Moreover, it was surrounded by a great ditch, wherein flowed the salt waters of the ocean. Hence, we may infer that the sea had not much ado to encroach on so confiding a city ...*
>
> *The Brahmans declare that this terrible overflow of the mighty waters was sent to punish the impious Ravana, who had dared to fight against Rama, the peerless king and warrior. Further calamities befell the isle about the year BC 306, when much of the west coast was submerged.*

When the sea, off the coast of Dondra is viewed on Google Maps, a rocky feature is seen in the sea near the lighthouse where the waves break. If this was part of a reef, the waves would break in a line, but they break in a limited spot. Is this a rock outcrop or the site of a former temple?

A parallel to Dondra is the Indian town of Mahabalipuram, also known as Mamallapuram. It is located about 60 km south of Chennai in Tamil Nadu. The Pallava dynasty who were ruling this part of the country started building many stone temples here in the seventh century. They built stone Rathas (temples in the form of chariots), stone Mandapas (cave sanctuaries), Rock reliefs and an eighth century stone temple called the Shore Temple (see Fig. 26). This temple was one of the first structural stone temples in South India and was located on a promontory on the seashore. The main deity in the temple is Siva.

Fig. 26: 8th century Shore Temple, Mahabalipuram, Tamil Nadu (Courtesy Wikimedia Commons)

There was a legend circulating for many centuries that this temple was one of seven temples, but there was no trace of the other six temples. All this changed with the December 2004 Tsunami. When the tsunami occurred, at first the sea pulled back about 500 metres, before returning as the tsunami wave. When the sea pulled back, onlookers were amazed to see a long wall on the sea bed about 300 metres offshore. A stone lion and elephant relief were also uncovered when sand was washed away on the shore.

In April 2005, the Archaeological Survey of India and the Indian Navy used sonar technology to investigate the sea bed opposite the Shore Temple. The wall that was seen by onlookers during the tsunami was found to be a stone wall six feet high and seventy metres long and was part of a temple wall. The investigators also located the remains of two stone temples and one cave temple within 500 metres of the shore. Subsequently archaeologists found the remains of yet another Pallava era temple. The legend of the seven temples came true after several centuries. It appears that there had been a severe tsunami in the 13th century which had caused considerable damage in this location. A picture of one of the sites of the submerged temple ruins which became visible after the tsunami washed off all the sand over it can be seen in Fig. 27.

Fig. 27: Remains of Submerged Temple, Mahabalipuram, Tamil Nadu (Courtesy Wikimedia Commons)

Did what happened in Mahabalipuram also happen similarly in Dondra submerging a temple?

There are three possible sites for the legendary Thondeswaram Temple of Siva. The first possibility is at the site of the Gal-gé stone temple, the second is at the main temple complex and finally it could have been by the seashore or even engulfed by the advancing sea. It is also possible that there were two Sivan Temples. This book presents the available evidence for the three sites. A final determination can only be made by further site investigation and off-shore exploration.

Anuradha Seneviratna was formerly a Professor in the University of Peradeniya and Head of the Department of Sinhala. What he wrote about Polonnaruva in the introduction to his book *Polonnaruva: Medieval Capital of Sri Lanka* applies equally appropriately to Devinuwara:

> "*With Buddhist and Hindu shrines in the same grounds embracing a common architectural tradition ...* (it) *was a city that symbolised the unity and integrity of the island as well as the religious and ethnic harmony which prevailed in medieval Sri Lanka.*"

Notes:

1. **Navaratnam, C S,** 1964, *A Short History of Hinduism in Ceylon,* Jaffna, p 52.
2. **Paranavitana S,** 1953, The Shrine of Upulvan at Devundara, *Memoirs of the Archaeological Survey of Ceylon, Volume VI,* Colombo, p 7.
3. Ibid, p 7.
4. Ibid, p 9.
5. **Ayrton, E R**, Antiquities in the Southern Province, Diary of the late Mr E R Ayrton, Archaeological Commissioner of Ceylon, with notes by John M Senaveratna, *Ceylon Antiquary and Literary Register, Vol VI, Part 4, April 1921, p 197.*
6. **Paranavitana**, pp 7-8.
7. **McKenzie, Capt. C,** Remarks on some Antiquities on the West and South Coasts of Ceylon; written in the year 1796, *Asiatic Researches, Volume VI,* London, 1801, p 454.
8. Official Web site of the Devinuwara Sri Vishnu Devalaya, www.devinuwara.org/shrine.html, accessed on 24 July 2007.
9. **Paranavitana**, p 15.
10. Ibid, p 38.
11. Ibid, p 11.
12. **Forbes, Major J**, 1841, *Eleven years in Ceylon, Vol. 2,* 2nd edition, London, p 177.
13. **Pridham**, C, 1849, *An Historical, Political and Statistical Account of Ceylon and its Dependencies,* London, p 595.
14. **Ayrton, E R**, Antiquities in the Southern Province, Diary of the late Mr E R Ayrton, Archaeological Commissioner of Ceylon, with notes by John M Senaveratna, *Ceylon Antiquary and Literary Register, Vol VI, Part 4, pp 191-193, April 1921.*
15. **Seneviratna, S**, 1978, Rama and Ravana: History, Legend and Belief in Sri Lanka, *Ancient Ceylon,* p 231.
16. **Gordon Cumming, C F**, 1893, *Two Happy Years in Ceylon,* London, p 449.

APPENDIX A

Thondeswaram Dance Drama
A free translation of the Tamil Lyrics

Scene: Thondeswaran Temple courtyard.

Narrator: An old devotee laments about the destruction of the temple and shares this nostalgic memory with a sympathetic listener. At the end, the listener consoles the old lamenting devotee with the hope that the temple will be restored to its former glory.

Old Devotee: Oh God, may I pray at your holy shrine?

(Green saree) You, who bless those who homage pay to you,
Tripura Sundari's consort divine.
I'm yearning for your compassion, so you
Must pay heed to my endless suffering,
And will you not grant me some graces few?
You are the Lord, I am your devotee,
Turn not a deaf ear to my humble plea,
When will you shower blessings onto me?

Listener: List'ning to your sad song, Oh devotee,

(Red saree) I was so moved, my heart was deeply touched.
Share with us your mournful melancholy.
The devotee looks up with affection,
And rising slowly to his full height, starts
Praising the glory of Thondeswaran.

Note: A sequence of pure dance by the Listener follows

Old Devotee: Haven't you heard of Thondeswaram of yore?

(Green saree) The Sivan temple with towers beauteous
And its sacred, sprawling buildings galore.
Our ancestors here prayed in ancient days.
Six times daily were poojas held, and they
Sang and danced, lauding you in many ways.

Note: A short dance sequence by the ensemble, followed by a Siva pooja are enacted at this point.

Old Devotee: The storm tossed sailors safely guiding light,

(Green Saree) The sea-shore temple's mighty gopuram,
Beacon for vessels on the ocean's might.
Now hear the story of how this temple,
Was destroyed by men zealously evil,
And then your heart will surely tremble.

The sturdy Lingam, full of tranquil grace,
The Nandhi patiently chewing the cud,
Mute witnesses in this sacrosanct place.
The stories we have heard resemble dreams.
One day surely these dreams will come true,

The lost glory will be restored, it seems!

Listener: Faith can't be ignored, it's not a surprise

(Red saree) Say the four Vedas; you can be sure that
Thondeswaram will, like a phoenix rise.
That much is truly certain. So until then,
Devoted holy one, peace be unto you,
And by His grace this must surely happen.

Amaithee, Amaithee.

(The assistance of Mrs P Sundaralingam in this translation is gratefully acknowledged.)

APPENDIX B

Alternative names for Thondeswaram (Devinuwara) over the ages

Name	Remarks
Dagana	Ptolemy
Deandere	Dutch
Detanavare	Portuguese
Deuanuuere	Portuguese
Deundara	
Deva-nagara	Pali
Dewa-nagara	Pali
Devapura	
Devinoor	
Devinuvara	Literary Sinhala
Devinuwara	Present day official name
Devundara	Modern Sinhala
Devundrai	Tamil
Dewundara	Modern Sinhala
Dewunuwara	Elu
Dinavur	Portuguese ?
Dondera	
Dondra	Anglicized name in British era
Duranura	
Girihelapura	Paravi Sandesa
Giriyala	Old Sinhala
Janura	
Nagarisa	
Tanauare	Portuguese
Tanavarai	Tamilized
Tanavare	Portuguese
Tandesvaram	P E Pieris
Tenavarai	Tamilized
Tenavaram	Tamil
Tendiratota	Old Sinhala
Te-nuvara	Sinhala form
Thennavanthurai	Tamil
Thenthurai	Tamil
Thevanthurai	Tamil
Thondeeshwaram	Tamil

Thondeswaram – Devinuwara - Dondra

Thondeswaram	Tamil

26489268R00063

Printed in Great Britain
by Amazon